# CHRISTIAN COUNTER CULTURE

*The man that is will shadow*
*The man that pretends to be.*

—T. S. Eliot
Choruses from *The Rock*, VI

# CHRISTIAN COUNTER CULTURE

## CHESTER A. PENNINGTON

ABINGDON PRESS
NASHVILLE   NEW YORK

*Library of Congress Cataloging in Publication Data*

*Pennington, Chester A.*
   *Christian counter culture*
   *Includes bibliographical references.*
   *1. Apologetics–20th century. I. Title.*
*BT1102.P37*          *239*          *72-13776*

*ISBN 0-687-07063-5*

MANUFACTURED BY THE PARTHENON PRESS AT
NASHVILLE, TENNESSEE, UNITED STATES OF AMERICA

To Andrew
our first grandchild
— and his generation —
with unyielding hope

# CONTENTS

# I. A Fighting Minority
## (Maybe a counter counter-culture?)

> No school [of modern thought] asks how it is that an essentially good man could have produced corrupting and tyrannical political organizations or exploiting economic organizations, or fanatical and superstitious religious organizations.
>
> —Reinhold Niebuhr[1]

If we are at all conscientious, we can hardly help being confused in today's world—especially if we are interested in being reasonably Christian. What on earth is going on anyhow? How can we find our way among all the claims and counterclaims that are being made? Is there a distinctively Christian way to understand, evaluate, and choose among competing interpretations?

### "Why does everything go to hell?"

It seems reasonable to admit that something has gone wrong with our civilization. How serious this may be,

11

what its causes are, and how it may be handled—these are troubled and troublesome issues. Lewis Mumford, who is usually restrained, learned, objective, simply exclaims at one point, "During the last generation the very bottom has dropped out of our life."[2] Many people, of more modest intellectual stature, would echo his judgment.

The problem, we sense, may be more than just immediate. We'd like to brush the suspicion aside. But even we short-memoried Americans recall enough history to suggest that our troubles may be more persistent than we want to admit.

Not long ago I was privileged to observe a discussion among some of the ablest thinkers in the United States. They talked learnedly, and with obvious frustration, about the complex issues confronting our civilization.

Suddenly one scholar burst out in exasperation, "Why does everything have to go to hell!"

He was not voicing simply a momentary annoyance. He was expressing a deep, troubled suspicion that something always seems to go wrong in human history. His outburst was not just a complaint against reality, but a plea that we try to discover why it may be true that everything always goes to hell.

In a way, I'd like to raise such a question and invite you to examine the issues involved. I do this unabashedly from a Christian perspective. I happen to believe that the Christian faith has a few ideas about what's happening, and why, and how we may recover our balance and sense of direction. Unfortunately, I don't know

12      *Christian Counter Culture*

any way to make such a discussion simple and easy, because the issues themselves are neither simple nor easy.

As I sometimes say to inquiring but puzzled friends, "If you ask complicated questions, you must expect complicated answers." There are few more complicated questions than those we must address to our contemporary society.

"What's going on?"

"How did we get here?"

"How do we get from here to where we want to be?"

"And how do we know where we want to be?"

## Culture, counter culture, sub-cultures

We begin where we are—that seems obvious enough. Where we are is expressed in our dominant, conventional culture. The establishment, as it is unflatteringly called, is shaken but not yet shattered. Just because it has survived and is present to us, it lays a certain claim on our support.

But our customary ways of doing things are being seriously challenged by an interesting assortment of what are known as counter cultures or sub-cultures. These may vary from rather simple and direct criticism of the institutions of society to quite complex efforts at alternate life styles. They all agree, however, that the present establishment is hopelessly inadequate to today's needs and must be replaced with something better.

As we try to understand and evaluate these alternatives, we find ourselves in an awkward position, espe-

cially if we happen to be Christians, and even more especially if we happen to be members of the church. We are
likely to find ourselves uncomfortable with all the alternatives.

On the one hand, the established culture wants Christianity to give its blessing to, and the church to act as
chaplain of, the status quo. Sometimes the church seems
content to serve in this capacity. But authentic Christianity keeps breaking through and upsets the church's
equilibrium. Christians are compelled to address the establishment "prophetically," as they call it, that is,
judging it in the light of their understanding of the divine
will. This, in turn, makes the establishment uncomfortable, and it tries to keep the church in its place, that is,
where the establishment wishes it would stay.

On the other hand, the sub-cultures take an ambiva-
lent stand with respect to organized Christianity, when,
indeed, they pay it any attention at all. They commonly
regard the church as a tool of the establishment and
soundly criticize it as complying with convention. Yet
these same sub-cultures will also condemn the church for
failing to champion their own particular enthusiasms. If
they criticize the church for supporting the institutions of
society, they also criticize it for not supporting their alternatives. They too would welcome the church's blessing, even while they reject everything the church stands
for.

So it happened, not long ago, that I ran, all unknow-
ing, into a nest of young Marxists whose primary criticism of the church was that it is not committed to the

Marxist ideology. When I suggested that Christianity cannot be identified with any ideology, they scornfully rejected the idea. Just as scornfully, I should add, as the typical right-winger dismisses the suggestion that Christianity is not to be identified with laissez-faire capitalism!

It seems never to occur to any of these people, no matter how radical or reactionary, that maybe Christianity consists of a few central convictions which cannot easily be compromised. That maybe Christians have pledged their allegiance to a Person who does not casually allow them to commit themselves to assorted ideologies. That the church may itself constitute a kind of counter culture which must stand over against any culture and indeed any other sub-culture.

Frankly, this is what I suspect is true. The following chapters have grown out of my efforts to pursue this hunch.

### A common thread

Such a pursuit of such a hunch required first that I come to a more adequate understanding of the various points of view which are being seriously championed today. In current studies and comments, certain names recur as being the most influential thinkers who are shaping these sub-cultural movements. As I read the works of these thinkers, I began to understand where young people are picking up many of the current "radical" ideas.

I realized more clearly than ever before that youth does not invent its own sub-culture. Students simply buy certain ideas which are offered in the intellectual market-place. The purveyors of these ideas are their teachers; this is true even of the youth who have dropped out of the formal academic scene. The teachers of these teachers are the writers of a half-dozen important books—which, by the way, you will discover being referred to in the following chapters.

Moreover, I began to realize that, if the Christian point of view is to be intelligently understood and advocated, we must know something about what these influential teachers are teaching. And—we must be willing to learn from them too. If we are going to be honest, we can't assume that we have the answers before we have fairly examined the questions—and other answers.

Then a funny thing happened to me on the way to this goal. I discovered a basic belief common to every one of these serious works. At the same time, I recognized that this common assumption is quite contrary to classic Christian belief. Here is where the issue between Christianity and contemporary civilization may properly be joined. Here is the point at which Christians will find themselves ill at ease, not only with our dominant culture, but with every counter culture seriously proposed on the current scene.

The belief shared by conventional culture and by every sub-culture is confidence in the basic goodness of human nature. An optimistic view of humanity runs through almost every serious study of the human creature and his civilizations. The most influential teachers of our time believe in what has been called "the perfectibility of man." Indeed, I would guess that this is what most people believe, or want to believe.

Frankly, I was surprised at this discovery. I suppose I shouldn't have been. My training in Christianity has led me to expect such a point of view to be the dominant one. Nonetheless, I was surprised. And just to indicate how pervasive this persuasion is, let me document it.

Herbert Marcuse must be one of the most prominent teachers in our society today. *Eros and Civilisation* is one of his most popular works. In a "political preface" to the second edition of this volume he confesses ruefully that his original work had been based on his optimistic image of man—"man intelligent enough and healthy enough to dispense with all heroes and heroic virtues, man without the impulse to live dangerously, to meet the challenge; man with the good conscience to make life an end-in-itself, to live in joy without fear."[3] I can only wonder that a scholar whose thought is the fruit of the unlikely marriage of Marx and Freud could persist in such a naïve view of humanity.

But then, this is a typical Marxian point of view. So Charles Reich, in his once best-selling book, comments that "it is now possible to believe in the goodness of man. . . . Technology has made possible that 'change in human nature' which has been sought so long but could not come into existence while scarcity stood in the way. It is just this simple: where there is enough food and shelter for all, man no longer needs to base his society on the assumption that all men are antagonistic to one another."[4] Again here is the strangely naïve notion that, once there is enough for everybody, human beings will live together in harmony.

Optimism becomes almost romantic when Theodore Roszak concludes his positive construction of a new religion for our new world with an exclamation that "the great purpose of life" is "to approach with song every object we meet."[5]

Even so wise and learned a scholar as Lewis Mumford, though chastened by his knowledge of history, cannot quite surrender his humanistic optimism. He identifies the theme of his most recent work as "Let Man Take Over." And he concludes his massive study of our civilization with the hope that "the gates of the technocratic prison will open automatically, despite their rusty ancient hinges, as soon as we choose to walk out."[6]

A most brilliant work of a member of the student generation repeats the same basic optimism. In his impressive study, Mark Gerzon explicitly rejects what he calls "the idea of the basic evilness of man," which he thinks conventional Christianity teaches. He sees the "unrepressed human being" as "a compassionately loving individual, not the basically evil character depicted by the Protestant ethic."[7] So he reveals not only a fundamental optimism but also a rather serious misunderstanding of what Christianity teaches about our human condition.

Even as I pile up the evidence on these pages, I groan within myself. Why does no one ask the crucial question? It is the question which Christian faith has always tried to force us to confront. "No school [of modern thought] asks how it is that an essentially good man could have

18     *Christian Counter Culture*

produced corrupting and tyrannical political organizations or exploiting economic organizations, or fanatical and superstitious religious organizations."[8]

## In pursuit of a Christian stance

Well, somebody has to ask such questions. They are difficult and unpopular questions which promise to yield difficult and unpopular answers. But the issue seems clear. I invite you to join the inquiry.

> "Why does everything go to hell?"
> What's really going on in our civilization?
> What kind of creatures are we anyway?
> Where do we want to go—and how do we get there?

If we pursue these questions from a Christian perspective, we will collide and conflict with just about every point of view which is seriously present on the scene today. If you like a good fight, you will enjoy this. If you're a natural-born compromiser (like me), you won't enjoy it at all. But if you're committed to the Christian faith, it's the only way to go.

After all, the church isn't in a popularity contest. It can't judge its ideas by their popular appeal. There are a few objective Christian criteria to which we have to be faithful. Then there are additional subjective evaluations and interpretations to be made. So that Christians aren't likely to be in solid agreement even among themselves—except at one or two central points.

The church can't go around asking the various groups

in our culture to grant it permission to affirm its beliefs. If we allowed every such group to exercise its veto on the diverse elements in Christian faith, do you know what would be left? _____, that's what!

Neither can we wait until we can count on a majority vote. I doubt that we'll ever get one. What we have to do is to determine what seem to be the central, dependable insights of the Christian faith. Then we must apply them vigorously and honestly to the troublesome issues confronting us as individuals and as a society. After that, let the chips fall where they may. It isn't our responsibility to guarantee a majority assent. It is our responsibility to be faithful to what we understand to be the Christian point of view. We can probably count on being a minority, a fighting minority—a "saving remnant," maybe?

Something which T. S. Eliot wrote in his essay *For Lancelot Andrews* has haunted me for years:

> "We fight rather to keep something alive than
> in the expectation that anything will triumph."

Do you find such an outlook grim, or challenging? Doleful, or exciting? Personally, I find it both exciting and challenging. I'm quite willing to leave the outcome to the accidents of history—which are totally unpredictable, and to the will of God—which is almost wholly undiscernible. But because I believe in certain human values and divine verities, I must engage in the struggle for a new humanity and a humane civilization.

Any volunteers?

# II. The Killing of the Primal Father
## (What happened to dear old dad?)

> This generation had to grow up without the time-honored gift from father to son: a firm set of beliefs and guidelines to accept or rebel against. The generation joined Bob Dylan in his lament: "I've got nothing, Ma, to live up to."

—Mark Gerzon[1]

Did it ever occur to you that the generation gap may be an expression of some deep cleavage in our human condition? That the impulse to rebel against authority may spring up out of some profound compulsion within our selves?

For a long time, I have had a hunch that something like this is true. (Admittedly, the Bible has encouraged such a suspicion.) So maybe you can imagine the shudder of recognition that ran through me when I recently (and all-too-belatedly) discovered Freud's myth of the killing of the primal father. Here is a dramatic statement that the generation gap, the rivalry between parent and child, the challenge to authority, is the re-enactment of a deep conflict within ourselves, a struggle which has left a wound which needs healing. •

## The myth and its meaning

Let me summarize the myth as I understand it.[2]

Society may be imagined to begin as a sort of family, in which the father has absolute authority: he owns the women, he makes the rules. The sons can't stand this; eventually they rebel and murder the father. They are haunted by the guilty memory of what they have done, but they have to build some kind of life together—as brothers. Ironically, the rivalries and tensions among them are such that they have to find some new center of authority. Father is dead, but some new father figure must be raised. (Long live the King!) So they build a civilization, riddled by guilt, driven by the need for order.

Now don't worry about the literal truth of the story. Whatever Freud himself may have meant, his interpreters see it as a myth or symbol of our human condition.[3] It is an attempt to picture what is going on inside us and consequently also among us.

It is as if every one of us is haunted by the ineradicable memory of some primordial crime. We have rejected an authority which was right and good. We have rebelled against a person who really cared about us. We had to do it. But we hurt ourselves in doing it. We suffer from a wound which must be healed.

**This is where we come in**

Now watch what happens. As I mulled over this story, a strange new fact came to me—a truth which makes me chuckle every time I think of its delicious irony.

The son who has murdered his father becomes, in his turn, a father! The children who have rejected their parents become, in their turn, parents! And the drama is played again—and again—at ever deeper levels of intensity and pain. For the parents are now persons who were once rebellious children, still haunted by the guilty memory of their rebellion, and who may still be having trouble finding a dependable authority of their own.

This is where we come in! So let me comment about several matters which concern us, in the light of this understanding of our human condition.

The generation gap is the result of our fundamental need to affirm ourselves, to find values and purposes to which we can give ourselves. It is part of our personal development that we test, perhaps reject, any established authority which is present. But we hurt ourselves in the process. We rebel against persons who have a claim on our respect. We reject a love which merits our obedience. So we can't just shrug off this rebellion by saying it's only human. It is indeed human—but it hurts.

Moreover, the gap is further complicated by the fact that the people called parents are themselves rebellious children who must somehow learn to act like responsible adults. And how do we do this?

Here is where the mythic picture of a kind of nasty

rebellion against a primal parent has to be modified. We parents cannot pretend to be the ideal, unrivaled source of authority. We have been, in our time, exactly what our youth now are, rebellious children. And we haven't got over it yet! We seldom admit this out loud. But if we are ever to understand and perhaps heal our condition, we have to recognize this reality. We are self-centered children, having difficulty growing up.

On the other side, neither can the rebellion of youth be idealized as a pure expression of a noble yearning to be free. Youth's rebellion is profoundly what it has always been: the childish awakening of self-centered consciousness, the immature assertion of self-interest, the confused rebellion of a dimly sensed identity.

On both sides of the generation gap are rebellious children, of different ages. And the difference in years doesn't, by itself, make all that much difference. On one side are immature persons striving toward identity and self-realization and striking out against anything that seems to get in their way. On the other side are persons who have lived more years and taken on more responsibilities (such as children!), clinging fearfully to a threatened authority, but secretly knowing that they are carrying the scars of their own struggle into selfhood.

There are several miscellaneous reflections that grow out of this.

Not everyone literally becomes a parent. What about those who are single, unmarried, or married without children? I think the same basic portrayal of our human needs is relevant. We all are children who have rebelled,

24      *Christian Counter Culture*

in some measure, against parental authority. We all need to gain some adult understanding and management of the strangely mixed feelings of self-assertion and dependence which we carry within us. We all need a dependable, self-chosen authority on which we can rely, a purpose to which we can give ourselves. Whether we become parents or not, we still want to become adults.

This means accepting the continuing insecurity of childish rebelliousness and the conflicting need for a dependable meaning to life. Adults cannot pretend to have an authority which does not really belong to them. They are rebellious children trying to grow up. But neither can adults deny their responsibility to affirm values and meanings to which they are committed. That's one of the things it means to be an adult: to live purposefully, to affirm values, to inject order and direction into society.

Youth must recognize the responsibility of adults, even while challenging them. Youth may be reluctant to admit it, but—if they are to achieve maturity—they need values and purposes to which they can commit themselves. On the part of both adult and youth, there is a continuing need for the discovery of some responsible authority, some dependable meaning.

If the child wishes to displace parental authority, he still needs some sense of meaning and direction for his life. If he rejects the establishment, he must establish some new assortment of social values to sustain his life. If he won't listen to his parent, to whom will he listen? Huckster? Pusher? Exploiter? If youth can find no dependable meaning in the establishment, where will he find it? Ideology? Exotic religion? Anarchism? How will he know what to choose? Can anyone help him?

One part of our adult responsibility is to offer the younger generation some values and goals which we believe to be authentic. We cannot do this arbitrarily or in an authoritarian manner. We bear the marks of our limitations. But there is no denying our role, without disaster to both generations.

I find ample documentation for this continuing need in the studies of many of the ablest and most profound psychological writings of our time. "Honor thy father and thy mother" is not just an ancient command. It expresses a profound human need for a dependable authority, a compelling meaning to life. The denial of this need by any generation, youth or adult, can only be disastrous.

### I remember . . .

Two incidents in my own life illustrate the personal process in which we all are involved. I suspect that every person can recall similar crucial occasions in his or her own life. These are universal aspects of our common experience.

I remember an event out of my adolescence. I had quarreled rather noisily with my mother and concluded my argument by stomping out and slamming the back door. When I thought I was out of sight, I turned toward the house and, with the timeless gesture of defiance, signaled, thumb to nose, toward her my final rejection.

At precisely that moment, my mother walked past the

kitchen window—and saw me. I was frozen into my posture, no longer of defiance but of humiliation. I had thought to insult her but had succeeded only in demeaning myself. Even as a rebellious child, I sensed my shame.

Obviously, this was not the only time I acted nastily. Just as obviously, I did the same thing to my father as well. But this particular occasion stands as a paradigm of my disobedience not simply of parents, but of God. Pennington—Everyman—caught in the childish gesture of defiance.

I remember another incident which seems to evoke an echo of primal human rejection. It was the first time our first child said no to me. I haven't any memory of what the occasion was or what I had asked her to do. All I know is that in the mystery of her own self-realization, our daughter looked up at me with eyes which everyone says look like mine—and said no.

You will certainly understand that this was not the only time she challenged my authority. And you will surely know that our son rebelled with his own style of male self-assertion. But I remember this particular occasion with a special clarity and sharpness. I realized that this was exactly what I had done to my parents. A primal human drama was being re-enacted. On both sides, each person had his and her own responsibility to bear.

At that moment I sensed, more than I remembered, a still more fundamental human fact. That was not only what I had done to my parents. It was what I had done to God.

*The Killing of the Primal Father*    27

Both the remembered act and the primordial reality have to be reckoned with in my achievement of some measure of maturity. Don't let me ever forget that I am a rebellious child trying to grow up, a wounded child of God in need of healing.

## The cultural crisis

Now let's take a look at our cultural situation. What we have portrayed as a personal experience is infinitely complicated by the fact that we are also social creatures. Our personal development is influenced by our social context. The values and meanings which we choose are shaped and offered by our civilization. There is plenty of evidence that we are living in an unusual period of our history. The 60s and 70s may well be called a time of cultural crisis.

I have suggested that the recurring drama of the conflict between generations takes place on ever deepening and broadening levels. This process is already as long as human history, and as complex as our civilization.

Civilizations do not stand still. Each generation starts where the preceding generation puts it. If the struggle between them is a recurring fact, the circumstances embracing the struggle become more radical and ever more painful. There is reason to believe that in the third quarter of the twentieth century this process has come to a critical moment.

So Mark Gerzon writes, thoughtfully, "This generation had to grow up without the time-honored gift from father to son: a firm set of beliefs and guidelines to accept or rebel against. The generation joined Bob Dylan in his lament: 'I've got nothing, Ma, to live up to.'"[4] (The author rightly sees this as a gap between father and son. But the complaint is addressed to mother!)

I sense the hurt in that accusation—and wince, because it hurts me too. I confess my own guilt, when the eminent psychotherapist, Erik Erikson, suggests that probably the older generation did dodge its responsibility in this regard.[5] But I have to add more—not to excuse anybody, but to identify a cultural process.

This is not the first generation to be without "a firm set of beliefs and guidelines." In fact, several successive generations have been in just the same fix. Why is it that the present parental generation either has no such beliefs to offer or is hesitant to suggest them? It is precisely because we are living in a civilization in which, literally for centuries, traditional beliefs and values have been undermined. The process by which such values are challenged, denied, rejected is a process which in our Western civilization is already two centuries old.

Every student of our culture whom I have read, who has any appreciation at all of the philosophical issues involved, seems to recognize this. I could document it quite convincingly. But let me simply offer a comment from a current study of our culture and its youth counter culture. This comment is typical of such scholarly observations. Theodore Roszak speaks of "two centuries of aggressive secular skepticism," which has been "ruthlessly eroding the traditionally transcendent ends of life," without offering us any adequate replacement.[6]

Let's pause to look at what this statement implies. It says that for two centuries the dominant intellectual tradition of the West has been "eroding" the traditional values affirmed in our civilization. It has done this by challenging the religious foundations for such values. The skeptical unbelievers have been unable to inject any adequate values in place of those they have denied. So we have come to what the author calls a time of "frivolous abundance." This whole development is cumulative, I would add. It has come to a shocking crisis in our own time.

Sometimes I think "decadence" is not too strong a term to describe this period in our civilization. After two centuries of increasingly radical attack upon the values and beliefs which have underlaid our civilization, we have come to a time when it is very unclear what is good and bad, desirable and undesirable. When youth challenges conventional values, there is no adequate defense, because adults have already surrendered their significant commitments.

So standards of excellence in literature yield to obscenities and crudities which shatter human values. In art we are not sure what meanings can be portrayed—if indeed there are any meanings. In music we ask, What is the difference between music and noise? In sexual relations, we deny any sense of discrimination among varieties of sensual pleasure. Public fidelity and business integrity are weakened because we don't know whom to trust. The religious beliefs which have historically supported human values are widely considered to be destroyed by empirical knowledge and still more widely undermined by popular neglect.

Such a description of our personal and cultural condition suggests a deeper dimension which we are driven to consider. The Christian faith insists that there is a religious dynamic in our human condition which may prove to be more powerful than all the rest. But let's be quite clear that as we say this, we begin to sound like a counter culture. Most people are not impressed with the importance of this so-called religious dynamic. If we insist that it is a factor to be taken seriously, we ought to realize that we are saying something that neither the shapers of our culture nor the enthusiasts for various sub-cultures are likely to support.

## The religious dimension

The Christian faith affirms that our primal rebellion is not against a mythical father figure but against a real God. The authority we challenge turns out to be the divine intention for our lives. The love we reject is the undeserved grace of a creator who cares. The crisis of our culture is rooted in the progressive undermining of any recognition of a cosmic ground for our human values, any admission of dependence upon a divine source for our very existence.

There is a beautiful parable of our condition. It is the story which Jesus told about a rebellious boy. "There was a man who had two sons ...." (Luke 15:11-32.)

The story is so familiar that we hardly need repeat it. Perhaps simply commenting on it in terms of our present concerns will be more useful.

The younger son rejected his parents and set out to realize his identity in his own way. (Not murder but rebellion is the term to describe our self-assertion.) Nothing turned out the way he thought it would. Worse than that, he soon realized that he was destroying himself. He was losing every mark which distinguished him as a son of his father.

He "wasted his substance"—the King James phrase is really more beautiful and more indicative than modern translations. The substantive gifts and resources which made him a distinctive person were being wasted. He found no satisfaction in his alternate life style, whether "riotous living" or "mighty famine." Soon he was forced to engage in demeaning labor, which was insulting to all the values he had learned to cherish (a Jew feeding pigs!). His freedom had become servitude of the most unrewarding kind. He was hungry for all the things that matter most, and no one gave him anything.

(That is a faithful summary of what happened to "the prodigal son." It reads like a summary of current critiques of our culture. Doesn't this say something about the accuracy of Jesus' insight?)

The young man realized that he was destroying himself, but was saved by one remaining hint of his humanity. "He came to himself." He remembered who he really was, who he was supposed to be. He decided to go back where he belonged, to recover his true identity.

The Christian meaning of the parable is clear enough. Every last one of us has rejected his identity as a child of God. We all have tried to assert ourselves in our own way. It hasn't worked. We've insisted on doing our own thing without knowing who we are, indeed, while denying who we secretly suspect we are supposed to be. This can only be self-destructive. The marks of our humanity are easily blurred. Our gifts are fragile and easily damaged.

Freedom seems to be one of these fragile aspects of our humanity. It can be subtly betrayed; we can lose it without realizing it. Indeed, in the name of liberation, we can surrender our true freedom.

The easiest way to do this is to imagine that freedom means the liberty to do as we please. With all our proper concern about the institutional and "systemic" limits on our freedom, I am inclined to believe that the most serious danger lies in our understanding and commitments. Liberation is often interpreted to mean the casting off of all constraints. I consider this a subtle threat to genuine freedom. Interestingly enough, it is not a new idea, certainly not an invention of the mid-twentieth century. It is as old as human thought, and it probably entered human thought because it was already a conflict in behavior.

There is a long humanistic tradition which affirms that genuine freedom means the achievement of human graces and dignity. This comes only by the discipline of unruly and destructive powers which move within every one of us. If we imagine freedom to be doing as we please, we will soon find ourselves driven by these dark compulsions.

Such a word is not likely to be popularly received today. But this may be all the more reason why it needs to be said. We are in danger of destroying our freedom by our commitment to self-pleasing.

We are seduced to become addicted to a pleasurable indulgence and are soon in bondage to our addiction. That it is the popular thing to do doesn't increase our freedom; it only enlarges the herd.

In the name of freedom, we are encouraged to use obscene and crude language. We lose the liberty to enjoy the beauty and grace of well-ordered speech.

We claim freedom to engage in any form of sexual pleasure we choose, and we destroy our capacity to experience joy. In our surrender to "the tyranny of the orgasm," we lose the delight of ecstatic union.

Christian understanding carries the humanistic insight to a still deeper level. True human freedom consists in the liberty to do the will of God. He wills only our good, our fulfillment. He wants to free us from the constraints of guilt, rebelliousness, self-interest, which limit our freedom. He wants to release us into joy.

Serving as a member of the household certainly beats feeding pigs! Our real freedom is in glad obedience to a heavenly father. Home is where our joy is.

One of the happiest insights of Jesus' parable is that the marks of our origin can never be completely erased. We can never quite forget who we are and who we are supposed to be. If we are obsessed by the memory of our primal rebellion, we are also possessed by the memory of our origin. If the first haunts us with a sense of guilt, the second sustains us with a hint of grace.

The Christian claim is simple. We must open ourselves again to the reality of the God we have tried to deny. We must accept the authority of the God to whom we owe our very existence. We must seek to realize the intentions which he has built into our very being.

*But it can never be a simple return.* Too much has happened. Our guilt cannot be ignored. A trust has been betrayed. A love has been rejected. We can't just pick up and go home. *"The Dreadful has already happened."*[7]

Everything depends on who, or what, is at the other end. Hardly anybody believes anymore in a vengeful deity. But lots of people believe in an indifferent universe. There's nobody there to come home to.

Who's there?

Is anybody home?

We must not overlook another character in the story, the older brother. He never left home. He never doubted that his fulfillment lay in obedient service with his father. But it all was spoiled by his inability to accept his younger brother. The older man didn't reject his father's authority, but he couldn't accept the paternal openness to a mixed-up son. So the older brother, rather proud of his status and content with his behavior, actually broke the relation with his father by refusing to join the celebration of his brother's return.

Our lives can be spoiled as much by bad attitudes as by bad behavior. Both Jesus and Paul knew this. Both warned us against the destructive power of the assorted hostilities and false aspirations to which we are subject.

Then Jesus injects an extraordinary insight into the parable. The father did for the older son exactly what he had done for the younger. He went out to persuade the stubborn, proud man to rejoin the family. The father met the resistance and anger of the son with acceptance and love: "All that I have is yours."

There is no mistaking the meaning of Jesus. The Father against whom we have rebelled still cares about our good. The love we have rejected is never withdrawn but always extended to us.

In this lies the possibility of our healing. Our guilt can be cleansed by the acceptance of divine grace. The meaning of our humanity can be realized by acknowledging our dependence upon the source of our being. We can find fulfillment in allegiance to the divine will for our good. When we consent to live as obedient children of God, we discover genuine joy.

# III. The Root of Alienation
## (How can we ever get together?)

> No one can begin to think, feel, or act now except
> from the starting-point of his or her own alienation.
> ... Humanity is estranged from its authentic possi-
> bilities. ... Our alienation goes to the roots. The
> realization of this is the essential springboard for
> any serious reflection on any aspect of present inter-
> human life.
>
> —R. D. Laing[1]

"Sometimes I feel like a motherless child,
A long, long way from home."

Does anybody care? I mean, really care?

One of the deepest troubles from which we are hurting
today is our alienation from one another. Many sensitive
students of the human sciences agree in identifying this
as a major problem in our time. It is, I believe, closely
related to the primal rebelliousness which we have just
tried to understand. If we are, in fact, disobedient children, we can't help feeling at odds with those against

whom we have rebelled, since they really deserved better. We will feel uncertain about one another, knowing that they are similarly defiant. We may even be uneasy with ourselves, because things are not turning out as we had expected.

Alienation is a sense of being shut off from one another, guarded, protective of oneself, unsure of the other. We feel that it is difficult to make significant contact with the other person, who may be a stranger, perhaps an enemy. We think we'd like to achieve some such relationship, but we're not at all sure that the other really cares. I'm not as sensitive to you and your needs as I suspect I ought to be. And I'm pretty sure you're not too concerned about me. Alienation easily moves from uncertainty to suspicion to hostility. All of us have plenty of all such feelings. They touch every relationship of our lives: parent and child, youth and adult, male and female, employer and employee, citizen and fellow-citizen, friend, stranger, foreigner, enemy.

Just so you won't think this is only a personal idiosyncrasy, let me document the pervasiveness of this problem by citing three current writers who are not only popular and influential but also reputable and highly respected.

Theodore Roszak calls alienation "the disease from which our age is dying." Yet this social scientist insists that it is not primarily sociological or economic, as the Marxists would say, but that it is psychological, "a disease that is rooted *inside* all men."[2]

If this is true, the deepest inquiry into alienation is done by the psychologists or psychotherapists. Erik Erikson is among the most influential men of our time. He writes movingly of "the abysmal alienations—from the self and from others—which are the human lot."[3] As I understand him, he insists that these alienations are experienced at every stage of our personal development.

Perhaps we can understand, then, why the eloquent British therapist R. D. Laing bursts out, "No one can begin to think, feel, or act now except from the starting-point of his or her own alienation. ... Humanity is estranged from its authentic possibilities. ... Our alienation goes to the roots."[4]

"Our alienation goes to the roots." It does indeed. One effort of the Christian faith is to indicate just how deep the roots of alienation really are.

## Strangers to one another

First let's examine the signs of alienation, which we experience in two different ways: (1) broadly and extensively outward, in our relations with others; (2) deeply and intensively inward, in our life within ourselves. I should like to consider first the outward, interpersonal manifestations.

In society, our alienation shows itself as hostility and frequently as violence. Distrust and suspicion grow easily into hostility. If all of us are living by self-interest, however "enlightened," we have little reason to trust one another. I would guess that distrust is one of the most obvious marks of our life together in society. We are constantly on guard for fear of being taken in, de-

ceived, cheated. We develop elaborate legislation to protect ourselves against one another. The community of
persons whom we can trust is usually a small one.

Hostility easily breaks into violence. One of the unhappy lessons we have learned since the outbursts of the
60s is that violence has played a large part in our own national life. Dependable historical studies have docu-
mented this convincingly.[5] There's no use to pretend
otherwise. We have been a frequently violent people.

One of the grimmest chapters in Lewis Mumford's
recent study of our culture is his account of the opening
up of the New World. Courageous Europeans discovered, explored, exploited whole new "worlds." In every
instance, these potentially creative occasions were
spoiled by "Western man's unreadiness for cooperative
two-way intercourse—his egoism, his vanity, his reluc-
tance to learn from those he conquered, and not least his
calculated ferocity."[6]

That's quite a list! These are the fruits of alienation.
And ironically enough, this is the same creature whom
Mumford exhorts to do something better today.

Alienation as racism is so evident as hardly to need
documentation. Our black brothers are urging us whites
to become more aware of our unrecognized feelings of
superiority and of the subtle ways we enforce them in our
society. Every ethnic minority is trying to increase our
awareness and sensitivity to our racism.

Just the other day, a friend showed me a statement
made in 1829 by a spokesman of the American Indians.
Addressing the white audience, he said, "Brothers, I

40      *Christian Counter Culture*

have listened to a great many talks from our great father (apparently the President). But they always began and ended in this—'Get a little further; you are too near to me!'"[7]

We wince at that. It touches us where it hurts. How shall we overcome such estrangement? The movement from stranger to foreigner to enemy is all too easy.

Furthermore, what shall we say of the violence expressed in much of our "entertainment". For years thoughtful students have cried out against the crudities to which our children are exposed on TV. The violence of war is beyond measure. The violence of so-called entertainment is beyond comprehension. Our alienation from one another is not only expressed in such portrayals, it is extended. Who needs it? But how do we overcome it?

### "Lonely—and going nowhere"

The other manifestation of our estrangement is painfully inward, an aching loneliness. Again it is psychology and literature which tell us how lonely so many of us are. A song popular among the young admits, "I'm lonely, and going nowhere." Youth may be quicker to confess what we adults are more likely to cover up. We feel shut off from others, shut in upon ourselves. We reach out, but timidly, afraid of getting hurt; fearfully, afraid of not being wanted.

There are probably lots of ways in which our efforts to break out of our loneliness are expressed. But I am impressed with the presence of this motivation in much of our current sexual behavior. The meaning of our sexuality cannot be approached simply in terms of its capacity to give pleasure. This is true and obvious enough and a real value. But sexuality, more profoundly, is a longing for authentic contact with another person. And the sex act is the most intimate connection possible. There is evidence, then, that a lot of our sexual encounters are not merely attempts to enjoy pleasure, but efforts to break out of our loneliness and establish a "meaningful relationship" with another person.

I remember a novel written a few years ago, in which assorted sexual adventures figured very largely. I've never forgotten the author's perception that the compulsion which drives his characters into these engagements is "the loneliness churning beneath that gay facade desperately every awake moment shouting to be spoken, to be therefore shared." In the relationships between many people he perceives that "the common denominator is loneliness. . . . A momentary sharing of sex. And beyond that the infinite separation, the alienation."[8]

### At odds with ourselves

The deep inwardness of loneliness suggests what every sensitive observer or experiencer knows: alienation is not just "out there," in our relations with others; it is also "in here," within our selves. We are not just ill at ease with others. We are at odds with ourselves.

This inner estrangement is as complex as our troubled

relations with others. Racism, we have come to understand, however "systemic" it may have become in society, is within ourselves. We have learned prejudices and acquired feelings which we only dimly recognize, but which divide us from others who are "different." Sexism is an attitude we pick up very early in our lives, and it crops out in the most unexpected ways. "The battle of the sexes" is no idle phrase. Violence is only slightly inhibited by our "civilized" habits. We shriek at the crunch of bodies in "contact sports"; we thrill to the battle between the good guys and the bad guys.

We are creatures of many and conflicting feelings, which are at once our delight and our despair. Some feelings are rewarding and enriching; others are damaging and destructive. Usually they are all mixed up in anxious disarray.

What we would like to do is harness the dangerous feelings, release the creative ones, and order them all around a basic will to love. But we have to admit that we don't quite succeed. Our feelings are difficult to understand, let alone manage. We need a center around which to order our feelings, a purpose by which to guide them.

Obviously, we have to keep working at the issues which divide us in society. But it seems equally obvious that we will never bring any lasting reconciliation to our social relationships unless we can also find healing for our inner estrangement. If we are ever to get together in society, we must also pull ourselves together as persons. (I think we have to say, rather, "let ourselves be pulled together." But that's a matter for further inquiry.)

**The heart of the matter**

The Christian faith insists that there is a still deeper mark of our estrangement. In doing so, we again take a position which can be called counter cultural. Most of what we have said about alienation up to this point is acceptable to most students of the human sciences. Facts are facts, and there is no disputing them. But now we want to look at what we consider another level of experience. Many scholars will question whether what we are pointing to are indeed facts. But we cannot deny the witness of our faith. So we move on to a minority position— and not unwillingly.

The taproot of our alienation is not simply sociological or even psychological. Our estrangement is entangled in the roots of our being. Our alienation extends to the very core of whatever it is that makes us persons. Our human condition is ultimately and unavoidably religious.

Our deepest alienation is our estrangement from God. Every other expression of uneasiness or strangeness or hostility is rooted in a still deeper fact: we are estranged from the reality that sustains us. Christian faith interprets this as the consequence of our primal rebellion against our Creator. We have not been able to sustain the relationship of dependence, of obedience, which is our proper relation to our Creator. We have affirmed ourselves in a disobedient assertion of independence. Our life is pervaded, every fold and facet of our personality is affected, by an unshakable sense of alienation. We are strangers to one another and at odds with ourselves, because we dimly sense that we are alienated from the source of our being, our Creator, our God.

One business of Christian faith is to bring this primal alienation into sharp focus, so it can be healed. As long as we only dimly sense that this may be true, as long as we pretend it is not true, or deny it, our deepest and most desperate human need can never be met. We must know what our need is, admit it—and then know whether there is any cure.

In order to articulate this dimension of our estrangement, the Christian faith calls up an ancient and familiar Hebrew tale: the story of Adam and Eve. I know there are plenty of scholars who will have nothing to do with such poetic portrayals. To understand and manage ourselves, they contend, all we need is "a technology of behavior."[9] But there are other scholars who recognize that as we get closer to the core of human personality, we must describe what we discover by using figurative language, symbols, drama. The religious insight is certainly this: in order to identify the deepest truth about our human condition, we have to tell a story—a story about ourselves and God.

Some will shudder at the "unscientific" character of such an appeal to what they regard as an ancient folk tale. It will help if we can shake off the uncomfortable feelings which have gathered around our memories of this story: where and how we learned it, what it was supposed to mean, the dark implications that were hinted. Then we can use the story as some of us have come to believe it

*The Root of Alienation*     45

was intended: a story about ourselves, to tell us dramatically some truths which we could not otherwise perceive.

The story, in Genesis 2, 3, and 4, is too familiar to be retold. Let us rather reflect on it in the light of contemporary concerns.

The divine intention for us humans was that we should live as total, fulfilled persons: at ease with one another, in harmony with nature, and in communion with our Creator. Labor was to be productive and rewarding; nature beneficent. Sexuality was intended to be not only procreative but also sacramental, male and female finding wholeness in union with each other ("they shall be one flesh"). Communion with God was natural, unbroken.

But the human creature has a special quality which is his true dignity: his relation with his Creator, and therefore with all creation, is not compelled but must be freely given. Our behavior is not governed by a built-in system of controls called instincts; we must govern ourselves by our commitment to freely chosen values. Our obedience to God is not compelled by his overbearing will; we must choose to give allegiance to his purposes for us.

What happened you already know. Adam and Eve couldn't maintain the posture of loving obedience. They decided to affirm themselves by asserting their own will. Now don't worry about what it was they did. Contrary to popular imagination, no apple is mentioned. And there's no substantial suggestion that it had anything to do with sex. It is said that they ate of the fruit of the tree which was forbidden them. They just disobeyed what they knew to be the will of their maker. They distrusted the one they knew cared only for their good. They did what the rebellious boy in Jesus' story of the prodigal son did.

Now look at the consequences. Talk about alienation! Look at what happens in the story of Adam and Eve.

First of all, they are torn up inside themselves. They are ashamed. Interestingly enough, there is no shame in this story until after the disobedience. Adam and Eve were naked and unashamed. It is only after they have abused their freedom that they are ashamed of their nakedness. They cover themselves from each other.

Second, their communion with God is broken. They are afraid. They hide. They are driven from the Garden. From now on, communication with their Creator will be strange and difficult—unless they can find some way to overcome the hindrances.

They are alienated from each other. The awkward and strained relations between male and female are consequences of the distortion of their true, complementary relations. If there is any "battle between the sexes," it is not the divine intention; it is the consequence of our human defiance.

The human creature is estranged from nature. They are driven from the Garden. Childbirth is painful and dangerous. (The folk wisdom which calls menstruation "the curse" is no accident.) Man must win his living by the sweat of his brow. Work is indeed necessary, but it may also become dehumanizing.

Then in the next generation—murder. A brother kills

his brother. In this story, unlike the Freudian myth, the primal murder is fratricide: human against fellow human.

Now we're ready for history to begin!

Have you ever read a more complete catalog of our human alienations? From the religious perspective they all root in our primal estrangement from God. We may—indeed, we must—work at the various breaks and conflicts in our relationships. Human beings are hurting because of them. We are hurting—killing—one another by our violence and hostility. But we must be aware of and seek the healing of the deepest wound of all, our alienation from God.

How shall this be healed?

Is there a healer in the cosmos?

### The miracle of reconciliation

The Christian story doesn't stop with Adam and Eve. There is a "second Adam." With him a new story is told, a new creation begun.

Christianity makes an assertion which it is very difficult for us to accept—or having accepted, to hold on to. The God against whom we have rebelled does not reject us; in faithful love he continues to will our good. The God from whom we have alienated ourselves takes the initiative in attempting a reconciliation. "God was in Christ reconciling the world to himself." (II Corinthians 5:19.)

"The Dreadful" did indeed happen. But the Good News is that the Incredible also has happened. Let me try to depict this with a few reflections.

The process of rebellion and alienation, once begun, is irreversible. In history and the development of civilizations, its effects are cumulative, it compounds itself. In our personal development, we know ourselves to be estranged, but it is difficult either to admit it or to overcome it. We build around ourselves barriers of self-defense. In society, our violence and hostility are built into the systems and structures which govern our social life. Racism, class conflict, war mark every advanced civilization we can think of. As history moves, as civilizations become more complex, some things are improved. But these basic human conflicts don't seem to get any better.

This is known biblically as the *judgment of God*. He cannot prevent the destructive drift of civilizations. To say it differently, he maintains the moral order which supports the processes of society: violence is self-defeating; self-seeking is destructive; only cooperation and caring will support society.

Judgment is experienced in our personal lives inasmuch as the same feelings which shut us off from one another shut us off from God. The same inhibitions which prevent our reaching out to others prevent us from reaching out to God. The defenses we build up, the distrust we acquire, become barriers to our communication with God. We can't seem to break out of this circle.

We can't go home again. There's no return to Eden. The best we can do is to improvise some sort of life "east of Eden."

But judgment is not the last word with God, perhaps not

even the first word. The gracious insight of Hebrew faith is that God does not abandon us to our historical fate. He stays with us in history. Despite our self-will and idolatrous attempts at building civilizations, he continues to try to persuade us to do his will. He never gives up.

The great word is *mercy*. The Hebrews believed that God was trying to reach them in the events of their history. If he had to let their rebellion run its tragic course, he faithfully tried to win them back from their destructive ways. Like a shepherd, like a parent, like a faithful husband—God extends his mercy to his people.

The Christian faith carries this beautiful insight still further. God cares for us with a depth beyond our human imagining. Not only does he try to influence the movement of history "from the outside," as it were. But he comes to us, intimately, personally, in self-giving love. He catches up into his own life all the pain and tragedy of our self-imposed alienation, to try to heal our estrangement. He comes to us in disarming love, to try to break down the barriers we have erected, to slip past the guards we have raised, to reach us at the roots of our deeply felt alienation.

The word for this is *grace*. The living reality of this is Jesus Christ.

The real genius of Jesus is this insight into the character and purpose of God. He taught that God actively seeks those who are "lost" in their estrangement, and this is the way he carried on his own ministry. He approached all who were open to his outgoing care. When

50      *Christian Counter Culture*

challenged for his lack of discrimination, he simply replied, That's the way God is. And that is why I am here.[10]

It was Paul's genius to see the deepest implication of what Jesus said and who Jesus was. There's no reason to imagine that this insight came to Paul any more easily than it will to us. But once he opened himself to it, his alienation was healed, and he knew the reality of reconciliation.

As Jesus had before him, Paul reverses ordinary religion and affirms that God takes and keeps the initiative in trying to break through our estrangement. It is not God who needs to be reconciled to us. He is always the same actively caring God. It is we who need to be reconciled to him: we have put up our guard, built up our defenses, developed an unwillingness to trust what he is trying to affirm.

So "God was in Christ reconciling the world to himself." Our acceptance of this reconciling love opens the possibilities of a "new creation." This is no easy psychotherapy. Our hostilities and bad feelings are too deep-rooted to be easily healed. Nor is it an instant utopia. There's too much estrangement built into our structures to be easily dispelled.

But at the root of our alienation there can be deep healing. Hostility can be dispelled by the assurance that we are loved. Violence can yield to caring. Estrangement can be transformed to reconciliation by the miracle of grace.

# IV. The Revolt Against Reason
## (But what else can we think with?)

> Nothing less is required than the subversion of the scientific world view, with its entrenched commitment to an egocentric and cerebral mode of consciousness. In its place, there must be a new culture in which the non-intellective capacities of the personality—those capacities that take fire from visionary splendor and the experience of human communion—become the arbiters of the good, the true, and the beautiful.
>
> —Theodore Roszak[1]

"Come now, let us blow our minds." This is the title I first thought of using for the present chapter. The phrase "blow our minds" seems to epitomize the revolt against reason which is so characteristic of our time. The title, stated in this manner, echoes an ancient invitation from the first chapter of the prophet Isaiah, an invitation which is really what I should like to issue in this discussion.

"Come now, let us reason together, says the Lord: though your sins are like scarlet, they shall be as white as snow; though they are red like crimson, they shall become like wool." This is a fascinating statement. The Lord invites us to "reason together." But he immediately calls our attention to a subject which reason, as usually understood, would hardly touch: "sin" and its cleansing. Most defenders of "reason" would rather not acknowledge the reality of "sin." So the invitation carries a haunting note, either of unreality or of intimation.

The Hebrew instinct, I believe, is right. We must use our reason to consider the whole of our human condition: the alienation which causes us anguish, the rebelliousness which makes us eccentric, and the ways in which these hurts may be healed.

Admittedly, such an invitation sounds a little strange today. Reason is seriously discredited among the currents of thought which are most powerful and influential. Once cherished as the supreme human gift, reason is under heavy suspicion today.

Such suspicion goes to varying lengths. In some intellectual circles and in some counter cultures, there is a forthright rejection of reason. Some psychiatrists regard "madness" as a way of coping with reality (I suspect this will never become a dominant school of therapy!). Some youth reject the intellectual life as irrelevant and settle for simple pleasure. A recent magazine article on the subject states that "many intellectuals have even given up thinking—or tried to—as if it were a bad habit."[2]

There is a subtle irony in this, of course. To use one's

*The Revolt Against Reason* 53

intellectual powers to discredit the intellect seems a singularly self-destructive exercise. For a psychiatrist to praise madness as sanity seems a peculiar kind of folly. For youth to reject the disciplines of rational thought will surely prove damaging to their personal development and to their efforts at forming social groups.

What troubles me most about the current suspicion of reason is that it plays right into our native indolence. We are reluctant to think as carefully as we should. Thinking is hard work. In fact, it is a peculiarly difficult kind of hard work. Generally speaking, we avoid it if we can. I would guess that most of the troubles that plague us today, both personal and social, root in our unwillingness to think with care and honesty. Certainly in the field I know best—religion—I am convinced this is true. Organized religion suffers from the refusal of its adherents, both clergy and lay, to be as well informed and sophisticated about their faith as they are about many other aspects of their lives. In any area, those who belittle the importance of serious thought are forced to settle for second-rate ideas.

Nonetheless, we are undoubtedly living in the midst of a revolt against reason. We had better reckon with it. Moreover, there are some aspects of this revolt which are entirely valid. The best way to understand where we are, and perhaps where we should try to go, is to look at various facets of the current skepticism about reason.

I approach such an inquiry with a troubled sense of amusement. It is exactly at this point that we Christians stand in uneasily mixed relation with just about every position which is seriously and popularly advocated today.

As Christians we are likely to have points of agreement with almost every current challenge to the supremacy of reason: the limits of technology, the relevance of feelings, regard for the dimension of mystery. But we are just as likely to have serious misgivings about these points of view also. Our distinctive faith goes further than other interpreters are willing to go.

Uneasy with our culture, we are not content with any counter culture. Our faith compels us to stake out a position all our own. Let's see what develops.

**Technology on trial**

A serious challenge is being addressed to technological or scientific reason. In almost every field of technical achievement, miracles have become everyday occurrences: everything from putting men on the moon to putting new organs into old bodies. But there is evidence that we may have outwitted ourselves. By following uncritically wherever our technical ability has led us, we are threatening our very existence on earth. Perhaps the most dramatic illustration of this, at the moment, is the ecological crisis. We are polluting our living quarters because we can't shovel out the wastes fast enough.

Personally, I have to confess to a certain ambivalence in my evaluation of technology. We have succeeded in making life a lot easier and more pleasant for a great many people. This may be one of the distinctive achievements of our civilization, and it is not to be discounted.

The success is not universal by any means; we still have a long way to go. But we ought not to belittle the considerable advances we have made in enabling a large proportion of our citizens to live pleasantly and comfortably. We may have produced a lot of silly unnecessary gadgets. But we have also added a lot to our lives that we are hardly willing to give up.

A more serious consideration is the apparent fact that, in order to solve some of the problems caused by technology, we will have to use more technology. Cleaning up pollution, for instance, is a complex technological problem. The solution to it will produce additional pollution. How to balance off all the factors involved is a highly technical puzzle.

But it is not only a technical problem—and this suggests the basic error we have made and the valid criticism which is currently being voiced. Human issues are never simply, perhaps not even primarily, technological. Values and goals are always involved in human life. But these are not supplied by science and technology themselves. The basic error of our recent history has been to accept uncritically the promises offered by scientific advances, to move ahead unhesitatingly wherever technology beckoned.

The assumption that because we could do something we should go ahead and do it, has been an implicit value judgment of the technological era. "Bigger and faster are better" is a similar unquestioned assumption. Production for profit has been a seldom-challenged goal. All these represent basic assumptions about human values which technology itself can neither challenge nor defend. Technology needs to be guided by values and goals which the technological sciences themselves cannot supply.

Of course, scientific reason will not readily yield to this criticism. In many areas of our culture, the natural sciences are still regarded as the only source of truth. It is assumed that human problems will yield to technological solutions. If we can put men on the moon, it is supposed, we can surely solve the problem of racism or poverty. The claim is that the sciences can determine the goals as well as the means. So an article, addressed to engineers, appeals to scientists: "It is time that science, having destroyed the religious basis for morality, accepted the obligation to provide a new and rational basis for human behavior—a code of ethics concerned with man's needs on earth, not his rewards in heaven."[3]

It is exactly this presumptuous claim on behalf of technological reason that is being challenged today—and rightly so. Frankly, I'm not sure how serious or effective the protest is going to be. But the technological crisis has deepened. The protest is more eloquent and open than ever before. Concern about "the quality of life" is more general. Technology is being challenged to be sensitive and responsive to deep human needs and values. And where shall we find *them*?

### But how do you *feel*?

Perhaps the most eloquent challenge to the supremacy of reason comes from the champions of the feelings. Here again there is a wide range of opinion. Since Freud, psychotherapists have explored the deep regions of the mind where powerful and dimly sensed feelings are said to exert great influence on our behavior. Today few movements are attracting more attention than the various groups devoted to bringing out the feelings of the participants. I even hesitate to use a name to identify such groups, they are so numerous and so different. But they all seem to agree that our feelings are the most important part of us, and that the most serious question addressed to us is, "How do you feel about whatever it is we're involved in right now?"

Let me say at once that I believe this opening up of the whole emotional aspect of our being is an important and valuable movement. There's plenty of evidence that we have stifled our feelings, and that they have exerted a disturbing power in our lives which we have not understood. Or we have been embarrassed to express our feelings and have deprived ourselves of many of life's rewards. Anything which can help us to understand and free up our emotions will surely enhance and enrich our lives. I'm all for it.

However, I confess to real misgivings about the enthusiasts who suggest that our feelings are the primary aspect of our personality, the most powerful force moving our behavior, and that their expression is the most valuable reward in life. I just don't believe this is true, and I'll try to say why.

In the first place, to say that feelings are important is not itself a feeling. It is a judgment, a conclusion affirmed by the reason. Whether feelings are important, or how important they are, is not a conclusion one can arrive at by the feelings themselves. Feelings don't make such judgments. The feeling person does. He does it, not with his feelings, but with his reason.

A major purpose of therapy and of group experience is to arrive at self-understanding, an awareness of the many and deep feelings that are bubbling around inside the self. A major purpose of encounter groups—which are not intended to be therapeutic—is to bring the feelings into consciousness, into awareness. To expand our consciousness is to bring a wider area of our inner life into the reach of our intentional awareness, that is, our reason. Awareness is not a feeling, it is an act of reason.

Feelings are many and varied. They are variously valued. Some feelings enhance life and some are destructive. But I see nothing in the feelings themselves that tells us which is which. Such value judgments are not made with our feelings but with our reason.

Our feelings need some scale of values by which they may be understood. Understood and valued by whom? By the person who feels and who must use his understanding. Feelings need some goal to which they may be directed. Directed by whom? By the person who experiences feelings and who aims at goals. Where shall we get such goals and such values? Not from our feelings. Here we have to pull together all our faculties, our powers, and seek to become whole persons.

Now we're on the track of the deepest power of our personality, which I shall presume to call (flying in the face of current enthusiasms) reason.

### Getting it all together

Maybe what we need is a broader definition of reason. I have already urged that it means something more than simply scientific or technological thought. To restrict the term reason to the specifically technical aspects of knowledge is really quite inadequate. It is, in fact, a distortion.

Reason may be thought of as our capacity for bringing together all the different facets of our life and shaping them into a coherent, fulfilling whole. Reason is the power to bring some order to the confused feelings which we experience. Reason is our ability to give direction to our uncertain self-will. Reason, therefore, resembles what we commonly think of as imagination.

Reason is our ability to form judgments, to distinguish among values, to make decisions. Reason may even be the capacity to embrace a faith which reaches beyond the grasp of reason itself. To reason is to pull together all the powers of the self which are at our command, and to be, to act, to become.

Let me reflect on this understanding of ourselves as reasoning creatures, with a few miscellaneous observations.

Pascal commented, "Man is a reed, the weakest in nature, but he is a thinking reed." Pascal would be one of the last persons in the world to suggest that "thinking" is an exclusively "rational" exercise. Few men have known better than he how limited is the grasp of intellect, how courageous the act of faith.

We hear much today about "identity" and many phrases relating to the term. We hear that the grave question which confronts each of us is, "Who am I?" The man who is probably more responsible than any other for our awareness of this problem is Erik Erikson. In one of his works he challenges the popular form given to the question of identity (Who am I?). He sees it becoming a fad. He urges that the real question is, "What do I want to make of myself, and what do I have to work with?"[4] This is the urgent issue indeed. To ask it and to seek the answer demands the best use of our reason.

## Reason and religion

Interestingly enough, several different things are happening to religion as expressions of the revolt against reason. On the one hand, religion is being helped by the revolt. On the other, it may be suffering from uncritical kinds of interest.

The scientific and technological view of life ordinarily dismisses religion as a product of immature, dependent minds, a sort of make-believe to protect us from reality. But the challenging of this kind of reasoning is based in part on the recognition that mere technology leaves significant areas of our experience quite untouched. There is more to reality than the scientific method itself can discern. There is a mystery about existence which ought to be enjoyed. (I think that's a valid way of saying it.)

The intellectual and popular restriction of beliefs to what science and technology will allow (supreme presumption!) has resulted in an emptiness which must be filled with something. We try all kinds of sense-pleasing distractions, but they aren't enough. Man does not live by fun alone. We need some kind of belief too. So three interesting things are happening today in religion: the revival of magic and the occult, renewed interest in non-Christian religions, and the attempt to create a "new" religion.

The traditional religious forms of our Western civilization are badly battered. We have already indicated some reasons for this. Many thoughtful men and women of our time find it difficult to take seriously the claims of conventional Christianity and Judaism. They find it easier to turn to other varieties of religious experience.

One of the fascinating—though to me dismaying—aspects of this religious curiosity has been the revival of interest in astrology, the occult, and other forms of primitive religions. (I have to add here that I do not include ESP in the category of the occult.) This would seem to fly in the face of any reasonable consideration of reality. One has to ask whether, in our highly developed, sophisticated civilization, we can return to primitive ideas which are quite incompatible within a reasoned, orderly understanding of the world in which we live. We have to use our reason to test and evaluate such ideas.

There is more merit in the popular turning to Eastern religions, though here again there are serious questions to be raised. These religions, for all their value, do not have a view of man and the world which is capable of generating and sustaining the kind of civilization we have built in the West. It is no accident that science and technology have developed in the West and not in the East. The Christian faith views the world as real, orderly, and good because created by God, and man as the creature capable of understanding and using this world. (If he abuses it, as he does—that's another problem.) The Eastern religions view the world as unreal, illusory, and human existence as an illusion from which to be delivered. Serious scholars rightly ask whether such religions are really useful in our civilization, and vice versa, whether a technological society can be built on such foundations—as the Eastern nations want.[5]

Moreover, the Eastern ideas which are popular among some scholars and students are usually highly selective, heavily edited, generally without the Westerners either knowing or caring that this is true. But if we are to use our reason, we must ask, What are the principles of selectivity, on what basis have some ideas been accepted and others edited out? Generally, the answer will point to some values which are inherent in the Christian faith (itself already rejected!).

An illustration of this naïveté is found in the thoughtful volume by Mark Gerzon. Oddly enough, although otherwise very careful and precise, he is quite willing to say that a student can pick up valid Eastern religious ideas without any serious study of them. "Any contact with alienated hippie culture will introduce him to the East quite quickly."[6]

This is like saying that you can learn what Christianity really is simply by talking with some friends about what you learned in Sunday school. I submit that such a judgment is hardly the best use of reason.

The third alternative is to try to put together a new religion. Here again I think it has to be said that the results are not impressive. One scholar who has seriously tried this is Theodore Roszak. He rightly and truly recognizes that "the scientific world view" is insufficient. It overlooks or denies too much that is real. But when he offers an alternative it is an appeal to magic, to the shaman, to mystical ideas which really demand more credulity than historic Christianity![7] I can only wonder why we have to use our reason to devise a religion that is more irrational than conventional faith.

The answer, I believe, is precisely in a hidden dynamic which ought to be identified. When we deny the true God and turn to our own devices, the best we can do is worship idols of our own making. And the idols are many. In this case, the idols of reason: either nontheism or esoteric religions or new forms of mysticism. There are cheaper idols—those of the marketplace: security, success, status, fun—the list is endless. The person of reason, however, will not be content with these. He is right to seek something better. He is wrong only in his idolatrous use of reason.


### The commitment of faith

The Christian faith has always had a great respect for, and a healthy skepticism about, reason. This is a difficult combination to keep in balance—and Christians have often failed to do so. But it is a necessary combination and admirably suited to the crisis of our time. Let me try to outline some aspects of the Christian understanding of our ability to think.

Reason, unaided, cannot supply the religion which the whole human person needs. In thinking about our identity and the meaning of our life, we must be open in two directions.

Our reason must be open to what total reality offers us. The world which sustains us is constantly sending out signals which indicate what reality really is. We have to be open to them. According to Christianity, these signals tell us a great deal more about reality than our reason could ever have imagined.

Reason must also be aware of what our deepest needs are. Our rebelliousness calls out for forgiveness; our alienation calls out for reconciliation. Religion must be responsive to those cries, and reason attentive to them.

Christianity affirms that our deepest needs are authentic because they are signals from the reality which produces and sustains us. Because this is true, reality responds to our needs.

Roszak, trying to make up a new religion, rightly insists that we must have a "personal, transactive relationship with the reality that envelops us."[8] He probably won't admit it, but if you think about it, only a personal God is capable of such a response. Christianity stoutly affirms such a God. Our capacity and our need for love are signals that love is present in the reality that sustains us. Christianity affirms that God is, indeed, love. Our recognized rebelliousness and alienation cry out for forgiveness and reconciliation to be found in reality. Reality responds with the whole fact of Jesus Christ. God offers what we most deeply need.

We could never discover all this by ourselves. The full range of truth has to be disclosed to us. So sometimes, in the name of reason, we refuse to hear the signals. But if reason cannot by itself discover these truths, it may be the supreme act of reason to accept their disclosure. What Christianity offers to every one of us is a passionate commitment to a well-reasoned faith.

# An Interlude: Invitation and Summons

"A passionate commitment to a well-reasoned faith." That is quite a mouthful, if we stop to think about it. And that is just what I invite you to do right now. We really have been developing a statement of the faith all along. Now let's pause to reflect on what we have been trying to say. And if this reflection draws you into commitment, or into the deepening of a commitment already made— that's really what Christianity is all about.

To take this faith seriously is to risk having your life reformed, transformed. So this interlude is informal and unfinished. But it is more than an incidental transition. It is an invitation to commitment and maybe even a summons to discipleship.

A Christian understanding of our human condition has kept pressing deeper than most other efforts at understanding. I have suggested that our needs are more serious than is commonly admitted. Christian insight discerns a depth dimension of our condition that brings us right up against a reality which we identify as God.

The deepest dimension of our humanity is our relation with the source of our being, commonly called God. The most profound human problem is the distortion of that relation. Our most serious need is the correction of that relation. The most exciting hope of Christian faith, then, is the promise of the renewal of that central, creative, life-ordering relationship.

This persuasion is admittedly an affirmation of faith. Some of us would want to say that it is also a reality of experience. But the experience is inseparable from what must be recognized as a presupposition. I have not tried to argue the reality of God. After the fashion of biblical faith, I have assumed it and reasoned about our human condition as if God were indeed real.

But, you may ask, is this being "well-reasoned"? I should want to reply, in the present circumstance, yes. We who believe in God, believe that this is an eminently reasonable belief. It makes good sense. As we live it out, it all hangs together. Moreover, such a faith carries conviction to every aspect of our being and gives shape and direction to our lives. This is what draws us into "passionate commitment."

If you don't find this entirely convincing, there are other ways of approaching the question of the reality of God. Many thoughtful persons have written carefully about their faith, and some with real persuasion. Indeed, I have tried to do so myself, but cannot tell how persuasively.[1] I would encourage you to pursue such a route, if you are inclined. But I could hope that you might be willing to go with me this way too—as far as you can.

As we have pressed the definition of our condition, we have affirmed that God responds to our need in a way that can only be called surprising. I mean, if we hadn't heard something like this most of our lives, we never would have guessed it. Our surprise is dulled by familiarity. But let's not miss the truly radical quality of Christian faith and experience.

Our rebelliousness, we have said, is not merely the rivalry of one generation against another. It is our primordial denial of our dependence upon our Creator. Yet God meets our rebellion with an undismayed love. He wills to re-establish the life-affirming relationship of loving obedience.

Our alienation, we have insisted, is not just among ourselves, or even within ourselves. It is a basic distortion of our relationship with God. We are ill at ease with one another, and even hostile to one another, because we are estranged from God. Yet God surprises us again and meets our alienation with the offer of reconciliation.

Our pride in our own achievements, our trust in our own powers, causes us to assert ourselves against God in doubt and denial. Yet God opposes to our rejection a quiet, unyielding appeal to our sense of order and dependability, an invitation to wholeness.

Is this a "well-reasoned faith"? I should say, without any hesitation, yes. We do not—cannot—think ourselves into such a faith. But when we stand in it, we can think honestly about it and it grasps our reason, as indeed it seizes our whole being. We are drawn into "passionate commitment."

This central insight needs to be reflected upon still further. I have called it radical. It is really—if we can only see it fresh—shocking. It is intended to be. It is intended to shock us out of our conventional beliefs and behavior into the kind of existence which the New Testament calls "a new creation," or "a new being." (II Cor. 5:17.) (It really is a recapturing of the original intention of our being. But considering what we have done with the original, this re-newing is certainly a new act of creation.)

The striking, almost incredible insight of the Christian faith is that, in meeting us at the point of our most real needs, God seizes and keeps the initiative. He does not wait for us to recognize the full dimension of our need; he stimulates the need itself, so that we may sense its full meaning. He does not wait for us to turn to him for help; he comes to meet us where we are, so that our meeting may be the turning.

I find myself fascinated by Graham Greene's beautifully inelegant figure of speech. One of Greene's typically troubled characters complains that God is like an underhanded lover, "taking advantage of a passing mood."[2] Isn't this a startling belief, really, that in the twists and turns of our ordinary experiences, as well as in the crises which shake us, God is trying to reach us with his creative healing love!

How do we come to this daring faith? In encounter with Jesus Christ. This really is what Jesus Christ is all about. The deepest thrust of his teaching, the most searching aspect of his ministry, are precisely the proclamation and the portrayal of God's seeking love.

God, he said, is like a shepherd who goes out to search for a lost sheep.

God, he said with a smile, is like a woman who turns the house upside down to find her lost savings.

God, he said with real understanding, is like a father who rushes out to welcome a rebellious son. Indeed, he added with even greater sensitivity, God is like that same father who goes out to the other son, sullen, jealous, self-righteous, and invites him to share the family joy.[3]

Jesus not only talked this way; he acted this way. When he was challenged about the propriety of his actions, Jesus simply replied, that's the way God is, and that's why I am here. "The Son of man came to seek and to save the lost." (Luke 19:10.)

Who are "the lost"? Who, if not the rebellious and fearful, the alienated and angry, the proud and insecure?

And who are the "saved"? Who, if not those who have been found, who know who they are intended to be, who know where they are and where they hope they are headed?

This is why Paul is so beautifully right in using the figurative language of reconciliation: "God was in Christ reconciling the world to himself." The divine initiative is expressed definitively in the whole fact of Jesus Christ. In him God comes to us—always keeps coming to us—to win us back from rebellion, to heal our alienation, to give wholeness to our divided self.

Well, here we are—confronted not by a theoretical proposition but by a real Person, a Person who looks just like our Maker. The claim he makes upon us is not simply intellectual assent or a sort of good-natured agreement. He claims the commitment of our whole self, or at least as much of our selves as we can pull together as of this moment.

So the basic question we have to answer is whether we are willing to open ourselves to the healing and direction of the God who sustains us, who seeks us, and who wants to enable us to become whole persons.

Such an invitation is also a summons. It is a call to join a faithful minority. It hardly need be argued that the position we have reviewed in these few paragraphs is a counter-cultural faith. The majority of people in our time simply are not committed to any such view—and are not likely to become so. Moreover, the assorted sub-cultures that are current are not noticeably Christian, not in our terms at least. So we are staking out a faith which is also counter the counter cultures.

This is what it means to be seriously Christian: to be passionately committed to a Person who wins and commands our primary allegiance; to be excitedly persuaded of truths which are not generally acceptable but to us are inescapable. This is a faith which is distinctive, awkward, but compelling. And we believe it may also be creative.

There is another dimension of this summons. If we respond honestly to the love of God, we will discover that he wants us to care about our fellow humans. After all, God loves them, and he calls us to similar concern.

Another way of looking at this truth is simply to recognize the human fact that we cannot live in isolation from others. We need to live in community, indeed, we really want to. Our need for others is the human side of the divine command that we care about one another. What God commands, we deeply need. So the failure to live in harmony with others not only hurts them but hurts ourselves. The hindrances to community are marks of our failure to be truly human. The command and the need—and therefore the summons—is to discover ways to live together in genuine community.

So our Christian faith and experience impel us to participate responsibly in society, to live in honest concern for the good of our fellow humans. The faithful minority must be a fighting minority. What do we fight for? What do we believe is possible? To win? To keep something alive?

There is another whole range of questions to be explored. We turn to them now.

# V. Shaping a Civilization
## (Does it have to be plastic?)

> As soon as the human group arrives at what we can
> term a civilization . . ., it assumes concrete form as
> a city. . . . Civilization is expressed by a city. . . .
> The city is man's greatest work.
>
> —Jacques Ellul[1]

*Homo sapiens* is also *homo faber*. We humans not only
think, we also build. We try to put into visible or work-
able form what we have imagined. Chief among our creations is civilization. We cannot live without a civilization
of some kind. We have to build one. If it goes down, our
successors build another on our ruins.

"But does it have to be plastic?" That's what I hear
thoughtful youth asking today. OK, they say; so we have
to have a civilization. But does it have to be artificial and
phony and false, as so much of ours is? Why can't it just
be real? The question is a perceptive one, a troubling
one, and a tough one.

In response to the challenge let me stake out a thesis,
which we will examine and test further. Civilization is a

necessary expression of our humanity. The human animal must make himself a civilized creature. However, in religious terms, a civilization inevitably becomes idolatrous. Culture distracts us from the worship of the true God and becomes our idol. Therefore, the Christian attitude to our civilization—any civilization—must be mixed. We endorse its humane values and all that enhances our humanity. But we must reject its idolatry, which necessarily diminishes our humanity. The tension of this ambiguity is hard to maintain. But it is essential to a well-balanced life.

## The human builder

Civilization grows out of fundamental human needs and powers. We need to live together; so we must build economic, political, and social structures. Moreover, we have powers of imagination and creativity; so we must enrich our lives with the arts. Humanity does not live by bread alone, but by beauty also. The hunger for beauty is as real as the hunger for bread. The lack of bread may be more obviously fatal, but the absence of beauty can be just as deadly.

Any given civilization seems to be a strange mixture of values and disvalues. Take our own, for example. Technology, as we have already mentioned, has become a major mark of our society. This has brought us great advantages, many of which are not unmixed blessings.

Mobility, for instance, is one of the remarkable characteristics of our lives. Recently, given a three-month sabbatical, my wife and I were able to travel and study and work on three continents, from Hong Kong to Santa Barbara to London. This would not have been possible without jet travel. The opportunities for significant travel and for vacations are beyond computing. And what shall we say of the automobile? Not many of us can seriously imagine a society without swift wheels. Yet the fact of greater mobility puts enormous strain on family life, makes incredible demands on businessmen and politicians who must fly from time zone to time zone, to say nothing of the pollution all the instruments of mobility spew into the air.

Consider the mixed benefits of electrical power. Only some thirty years ago, there was a great national effort to electrify rural America. It was a sort of crusade, to bring the values of electrical power to isolated rural regions of America. The crusade succeeded. My wife and I recently flew from Washington to Minneapolis on a relatively clear night. Wherever the ground was in sight, the whole dark countryside was dotted with an unbroken network of lights. And what shall we say of all the ease and comfort which electrical gadgets have brought to our lives? Yet electricity has brought with it a change in our living patterns, the empty entertainment of TV and radio (as well as their real values), and how much pollution to our air and water.

You can think of your own illustrations of the mixed quality of our culture. The very success of our technological development has become a source of crisis in our civilization.

The city is recognized by many social scientists as the

epitome of civilization. "Civilization is expressed by a city. . . . The city is man's greatest work."[2]

Look at our cities! Everything that is good and bad in our civilization is crowded into them. They magnify and intensify every value and disvalue of our culture. The great art institutions are in our cities: museums, orchestras, theaters. So also are the sources which produce and promote the cheap pop culture which floods our nation. Philanthropic and service agencies flourish, but so does crime in all its most dangerous and degrading forms. Unimaginable affluence mixes with incredible poverty.

Most serious students of our society seem to agree that our cities are beset by apparently insoluble problems. Some are almost ungovernable; many nearly bankrupt. The crisis of our civilization is epitomized in the crisis of our cities.

A religious analysis of civilization will insist on pressing still deeper. The basic cultural error which we make is to turn our artifacts into idols. We place supreme value on our human powers and achievements. Our civilization becomes idolatrous. We value, that is to say, we worship, our own creations, rather than the source of our creativity.

Art for art's sake is a clear illustration of this process. The intense pursuit of creature comforts and sensate pleasures is another. The faith placed in political-economic power is yet another.

The Hebrew prophets recognized that idolatry is the basic and most destructive human error. It lay at the root of every weakness eating away at their nation. In anger and anguish they cried out against the folly of a people willing to destroy themselves rather than obey a God who willed their good. The prophets saw the hard unpalatable truth that in denying the true god, and turning to gods that are not really gods, the human creature succeeds only in destroying himself and his highest values.

Iconolatry always ends up in iconoclasm. The worship of our own powers is really self-worship, and self-worship is always self-destructive. Human creativity, enthroned, uses its powers destructively.

## The primal repression

There is a hidden dynamic at work in this cultural process which needs to be brought out in the open. There is a Christian interpretation of what is happening to our civilization. We should know what it is, what light it throws on our cultural crisis, and what guidance it may give us for our own living.

The apostle Paul first identified and outlined the process. As a first-century man, his understanding of it was limited, but I think we can show that his essential insight is true and powerful. The paragraphs in which he outlines this cultural development are in the first chapter of his remarkable letter to the Romans (1: 18-32). A few words of caution are in order as we approach the passage.

Don't be offended by his language. Many of us have formed unhappy associations with certain biblical terms (for instance, "the wrath of God"), and our emotions boil when we hear them. Keep cool, and try to hear what Paul is saying in the only vocabulary he had—which we have spoiled by bad interpretations.

In addition, read the passage—dare I say "existentially." I used to read it as if it were intended to be anthropology or history, and I was never impressed, only puzzled. Then it dawned on me that Paul is not writing as a scientist but as a man torn by profound experiences and inspired by insights too deep for easy words. What he is writing is not science but a highly personal account of what happens inside every one of us and, consequently, in our cultures.

The process may be expressed in a series of words: intuition / repression / idolatry / confusion / corruption. That's the way it goes. Let's look at this sequence of personal and cultural events.

1. We human beings know the reality of God by intuition. As creatures produced and sustained by the entire cosmic order, we have a built-in sense of the reality of our Creator. This intuitive knowledge is part of our native equipment (vss. 19-20).

2. However, we repress this intuition. The primal repression is not what Freud thought it is, nor even what some of his opponents suggest. It is the suppressing of our intuitive sense of God (vss. 18, 21-22).

This repression is a subtle act of the whole person. It is not strictly rational, for there is really no rational way to deny the reality of God. It is an act, perhaps unconscious or preconscious, compounded of rebellious self-will, a haunting sense of estrangement, and a proud assertion of reason. Christian faith sees this as an inevitable stage of self-development from which most of us never fully recover, and which sets off a string of cultural repercussions.

3. Idolatry is the first consequence of our primordial denial of God. We are so made that we must worship something, that is, we must put some value, some goal, at the center of our lives. If we displace the true god, we try to fill the vacuum with something else. The something else turns out to be an idol of our own making.

Paul really put his finger on the heart of the issue. We make images resembling man or birds or animals or reptiles (vs. 23). Anyone who has seen anything of the religions of the world, knows how true this is. In substance, we worship and serve the creature—technology, art, pleasure, security, you name it—rather than the Creator (vs. 25).

Voltaire once observed that if there were no God, it would be necessary to invent him. He was exactly right. This necessity is rooted in a basic human need. When people cease to believe in God, it has been said, they do not believe in nothing but in anything. In the preceding chapter we saw enough evidence of this in our own time to impress its truth on us.

This slipping into idolatry is subtle but also pervasive. It unleashes a whole pack of consequences.

4. Confusion follows hard upon idolatry, confusion as to our own identity. As Paul observed this, it shows up first in a mismanagement of our sexuality (vss. 26-27). With our current permissiveness, we are tempted to dis-

miss this as Jewish Puritanism. But let's look a little more closely and objectively.

If the Hebrew-Christian understanding of human sexuality is at all accurate, we may well expect our loss of identity to show itself first at that very point, what Freud called libido. This is the second most profound aspect of our humanity. First and most basic is the divine image which we bear, our relation to our Creator. But mentioned in the same breath with this is our sexuality. Let me refer to the creation narrative of Genesis 1, just to make this insight sharp and clear. "God created man in his own image, in the image of God he created him; male and female he created them." (Genesis 1:27.) If this is in fact true, it is reasonable to recognize that if God is displaced, the next most powerful aspect of our humanity will rush in to fill the vacuum left by his dismissal.

Frankly, this insight seems to me to make every bit as good sense as any thesis I hear being offered today. How shall we understand the strangely confused powers of our subconscious self? Or the fact that in every advanced civilization sex has been a problem? (Prostitution, pornography, deviant behavior have marked every advanced civilization known to us. These are no mere modern or Western problems. They are universal human problems.) How shall we understand the confusion of sexual identity and roles so evident in our own time? Can you offer a better thesis than this one? At the center of our self belongs a loving obedience to our Creator. If we displace this, everything else in the self is thrown out of balance. The center is then occupied by the adjacent, next most powerful aspect of our being. And who will deny that this is the libido, the sexuality which has been so dramatically disclosed in our time?

5. The corruption of our common life is the consequence of our primal eccentricity. Here Paul's list, if not exhaustive by twentieth-century standards, is surely comprehensive by any human standard (vss. 28-32).

All the destructive and hostile attitudes that spoil our interrelations and our social structures erupt from our idolatrous confusion. Here Paul mentions not only the physical misdeeds which are the favorite targets of short-sighted religionists. He mentions all the nasty, hostile, petty, destructive attitudes which give rise to repressive and exploitive structures in society: We are full of covetousness, malice, envy, murder, strife, deceit; we become all the things which we are not intended to be, "foolish, faithless, heartless, ruthless."

It is a devastating indictment. It reads like today's newspaper. But unlike the newspaper or most serious studies, it roots the whole human crisis in the primal repression of our intuition of God.

### Does it have to be this way?

The process we have just outlined appears to be inevitable. If anyone were to ask me whether civilization has to go this way, I would be forced to answer in the affirmative. This may sound pessimistic, but I consider it simple, open-eyed realism. I don't know of any instance in which it has not gone this way. Even the medieval civilization, largely constructed by the Christian church, became idolatrous. The church, ironically, exalted itself to the place which belongs to God. Exactly so. That's the way it goes, and it has all the appearance of inevitability.

If it is true that every civilization seems to have followed this route, it is also true that they all worship the same false gods. There are three cultural values that are given top priority in just about every civilization. They are pleasure, power, and profit. They may take different forms, assume different appearances, but underneath they are the same. I would guess that in any "advanced" or "decadent" stage of any civilization, we would find these values ranked high by those who determine the shape of culture.

We, in turn, have simply picked up the old gods and refurbished them, modernized them.[3] We are able to serve them with all the devices at our command: technological cleverness, persuasive, even manipulative, means of communication, commercial pressures and promises of all kinds. The old gods may be hardly recognizable in mod, psychedelic array. But strip them, and their resemblance is laid bare.

One complicating factor is that the symbols and practices of conventional religion also persist. The churches and synagogues are still in business, and indeed they seem to exert continuing, if dwindling, influence. The presence of these symbols may persuade some of us that conditions are not so bad as the preceding pages have suggested. I would say that we must not be deceived by these appearances. Things are at least that bad.

What happens is that the conventional religious symbols persist, but they really symbolize something that is hardly believed any more. "A personal God? Who actually became a man? And died on a cross for our sins? Really, now. . . ." Our earlier discussions have indicated that these historic beliefs are widely discredited today, even, I would add, in the churches which are themselves symbols of these historic beliefs!

Jacques Ellul, the French social scientist, has developed, with impressive power, the thesis that we try to build our civilization without God. Indeed, we try to shut him out of our cultural structures. The city, which is the supreme expression of a civilization, is the place in which we try to build our own style of life without God. The churches which remain are marks of a faith no longer seriously believed.[4]

The American novelist Peter De Vries makes the same comment about the church steeples which, outnumbered and overshadowed, mark the towns and landscapes of New England. He is troubled by his observation, because he sees the steeple as a symbol of a lost faith, a ghost which still haunts the house. He comments sadly: "The less you believe what it proclaims, the more you cherish what it recalls."[5]

Sad, isn't it? But true.

## Breakdown in communication

If you are still interested in myths as possible dramatizations of our condition, we have one for this cultural process. It's the old story about the tower of Babel.[6] (Genesis 11:1-9.)

Civilization had advanced—a second start, after the Flood—to the building of cities. A particular group of plain-dwellers decided to grace their city with a tower. "Let us make a name for ourselves," they said. That is, let us establish our own identity.

The same human error: unable to accept the identity which God confers on us, we try to make a name for ourselves. We use our creativity to exalt ourselves. We try to build our own community, on a strictly humanistic basis.

And what happens? A breakdown in communications: The sharpest kind of alienation among us—we can no longer understand one another. The real point to the outcome in the story is not that the people spoke different languages. It is rather that they could not understand one another. Their efforts at community came to nothing. They were "scattered," fragmented, estranged.

Isn't that exactly where we are today? Not only do we fail to understand one another. We cannot even trust one another. And the two may be inseparably linked. Nations spar cautiously and engage in the strange double-talk of diplomacy. But what is more double-talk than the average politician's response to a direct question? Motivated by self-interest, economic groups demand and threaten and push one another around. People of different ethnic and social backgrounds don't really understand one another. "What do they want?" they ask fretfully.

Talk about Babel!

Color it USA.

Somewhere, just recently, I heard the shrewd comment that Pentecost reverses Babel. At Babel the people moved from a common language to a confusion of tongues, in which they were unable to communicate with one another. At Pentecost the people involved spoke different languages, but they understood one another. Maybe if we could find our way from the Tower of Babel to the Upper Room in Jerusalem, we just might. . . . Just might what? The church, the inheritor of Pentecost, sounds more like Babel than the Upper Room!

**Toward a new humanity**

That final sentence reveals the major embarrassment of the Christian church today. We believe we have the right diagnosis and the right cure. But we don't seem to be able to produce enough healed people. We believe our analysis of the human predicament is accurate. We believe we have a transforming message. But we can't point out many people who look and act as if they have been transformed. If you test us by our results, we really don't have much to show for all our efforts. It's embarrassing.

However, we're just stubborn enough to stay with our message. It's even called a "gospel," which means "good news." We believe the good news is that, if we take our faith seriously, we can become healthy and whole persons. And as such, we may have some positive influence on our crazy civilization.

At this point, the ambivalence of our relation to our culture becomes apparent. As I said in the original statement of the thesis for this chapter, our attitude toward our civilization is mixed. We endorse and enjoy everything in our culture which enhances our humanity. But we must reject and oppose everything which we judge to be destructive of humane values. This puts us in a difficult and awkward position. We can never be completely at ease in any civilization. There is much which we gladly enjoy. There are values we want to strengthen in our society. But there are other practices which we must reject, and values whose popularity we must deplore.

Interestingly enough, I receive support in such a stance from two quite different scholars. Different as they are, both are agreed that what we need today is more men and women who will say "no" to our culture when it is "plastic," and say "yes" only to those goals and values which are truly humane.

Charles Reich in *The Greening of America* writes realistically of the Corporate State and its power over our lives. Somewhat less realistically, he depicts a new consciousness which is dawning over our country. But on closer examination, that consciousness depends on enough men and women undergoing a kind of "conversion." That is, he exhorts us to change our goals, our value systems, our world view, our "whole way of life." We must reject the values being pressed on us by the Corporate State and choose "a new life-style." "Revolution by consciousness" is really revolution by the decisive action of a determined minority. It requires the courageous decision to live by values and standards and goals of our own choosing.[7]

In *The Pentagon of Power,* a work of infinitely greater scholarship, Lewis Mumford issues a remarkably similar exhortation. From the beginning of this profound study he has acknowledged that the crisis of our culture is fundamentally a religious crisis. He speaks repeatedly of the need for a new "world picture," even "something like a spontaneous religious conversion." Then, in a witness to his own experience, he invites us to detach ourselves from the system "and to make a selective use of its facilities."[8]

I read these words with a strange shock of recognition. That's exactly the way I had learned Christianity! From my earliest days I was taught that Christians are willing to reject anything in contemporary culture that they think is dangerous or false, and embrace only what they believe adds to the grace of human life. We are to do this for Christ's sake.

For many years this teaching seems to have dropped out of sight in our churches. The Christian life has taken the appearance of mere conformity to the contemporary American way.

Now, much to our chagrin, and to our delight I should hope, we are being called back to the kind of healthy nonconformity which has always been the Christian way. We are being assured, by earnest youth and learned scholar alike, that this may be the best thing we can do for our disturbed civilization.

Let's get at it, for Christ's sake.

Another way to put it, perhaps a little more authentically, is to say: Let's open ourselves to the possibility of becoming this kind of person. Not taking our values from a commercialized society, but from our vision of Christian humanity. Not setting our goals according to the pressures of conformity, but according to the perceived purpose of God.

There's a beautiful prayer in the liturgy of the church in which it is asked that we "may love the things which Thou commandest, and desire what Thou dost promise." If we could just let ourselves be transformed into such persons, we just might. . . . Just might what?

Just might find our way from the Tower of Babel to the Upper Room in Jerusalem—and from there to the street where we live.

# VI. Power Corrupts
## (What! even "the People"?)

> Modern democracy requires a more realistic philo-
> sophical and religious basis, not only in order to an-
> ticipate and understand the perils to which it is ex-
> posed; but also to give it a more persuasive
> justification. Man's capacity for justice makes de-
> mocracy possible; but man's inclination to injustice
> makes democracy necessary.
>
> —Reinhold Niebuhr[1]

"Man is by nature a political animal." That's the way
Aristotle said it, and no one has ever effectively disputed
it. We may take the statement to mean two things.

We human beings have a built-in need to live together.
The hermit is an eccentric. People need people. So we
live together in communities of many kinds.

Politics is the term we apply to the ways we organize
our common life. We need rules and regulations; we need
systems and structures. Across the span of history and
the reach of cultures, these political forms are incredibly

varied. But they all have the same purpose of enabling us to live together. Politics is the business of ordering our common life.

One further observation is relevant. This political animal is the same creature we have been talking about in previous chapters. All the factors we have mentioned before are brought into the business of politics. The political animal is still rebellious, alienated, proud, and idolatrous. All our human gifts and griefs play their part in our political experience.

### The name of the game

Power is the name of the political game. The central fact of politics is power: power to regulate people's lives and to force them to obey the laws; power to collect money by taxation and decide where it will be spent; power to put people into jobs and pull them out. The central task of politics is the ordering of power for the common good. The central question, then, is who has the power. The struggle is to gain power and use it for one's chosen ends.

"Black Power" is a slogan which has been variously interpreted in recent years. When used most carefully and thoughtfully, it identifies the struggle of black citizens to gain the kinds of political and economic power which have been denied them in white society. It is a struggle, because those who have power, whoever they are, are not going to give it up easily. We do not gladly share significant power. We have to be forced to concede it to someone else. That's why blacks have to fight to gain power. If we have any sense of humanity and justice, we will applaud their struggle, share whatever power we may have, and join them in their efforts to overcome the resistance which may still be offered to their legitimate demands.

If power is the prize to be sought, the greatest danger in politics is the collusion of powers. A coalition is able to manipulate political and economic factors for the benefit of the members of the coalition. The two principal powers in our society, I suppose, are economic and political. Any alliance between any combination of economic and political interests is a dangerous development.

For this reason a separation and balance of power is essential to a democracy. The United States, of course, was organized on such a basis, the separation of the various branches of government. What is more difficult to manage is the relationship between political and economic powers. A clear separation between them may not be possible. The welfare state seems to seek a coalition as much as the capitalist state ever did, even though perhaps for different purposes. A large part of political power seems to be the regulation of economic factors, to raise and distribute monies. The well-being of the economy has become a major political concern.

One of the serious criticisms leveled against our present American system is precisely that it represents an alliance of economic and political power in the interest, not of the general public, but of the present wielders of these powers. I take this to be the burden of Reich's criticism of the Corporate State. It is, he says, a coalition of government and industry, binding the nation into "a single vast corporation," of which every citizen is an employee. "The corporate state," he writes, "is an immensely powerful machine, ordered, legalistic, rational, yet utterly out of human control, wholly and perfectly indifferent to any human values. . . . The essence of the Corporate State is that it is relentlessly single-minded; it has only one value, the value of technology - organization - efficiency - growth - progress."[2]

This is the same critique being made—to a warmly responsive segment of our academic population—by Herbert Marcuse. "A comfortable, smooth, reasonable, democratic unfreedom prevails in advanced technological civilization, a token of technical progress"—this is the opening salvo of one of his most popular books.[3] Such a condition prevails, he claims, because "contemporary industrial society tends to be totalitarian." And this is because the combination of political and economic power makes possible "the manipulation of needs by vested interests."[4] Producers create needs, which may be quite artificial: as various as cigarettes, snowmobiles, and Sunday football. Then the economy gears up to supply these "needs." And the process is supported by a government which can stay in office only as long as it assures a stable economy. Such is the charge leveled against the present system.

I simply have to confess that I don't really know how true this accusation is. My friends who are in politics and business and law deny it. The evidence seems often to support the indictment rather than the defense. Who decides that we will pour billions of dollars into a space program? Who decides we will go into Southeast Asia—or pull out? Who decides whether there will be significant tax reform? Who decides which parts of our economy will be subsidized, how much and in what ways? Transportation, urban renewal, education, welfare—the issues are enormous. Who can disentangle the mixed interests that influence decisions in these areas? Some years ago, we were warned about the dangers of a "military-industrial complex," and that warning was not from a left-wing political philosopher. Since then, others have said it looks more like a military-industrial-labor-university research complex.

What I do fear is that, if we have in fact come to some such point in our American life, we are already endangering the democratic ideal to which we are supposed to be committed. And if we have not gone so far, we nonetheless must be alert to the ever-present danger of such a collusion of powers. One of the greatest of our American political philosophers, Reinhold Niebuhr, called this "the final peril of combining political and economic powers."[5] He is certainly right.

## Power corrupts

The reason for the gravity of this danger is simple. Power corrupts. This is a maxim which some of us learned during the second quarter of the present century. We watch with dismay as this truth is quite ignored in the seventies. For we have seen nothing in the movement of history from that time to this which discredits the assertion. In fact, some of us are inclined to say that everything illustrates its truth.

"Power corrupts; absolute power corrupts absolutely." That is the complete maxim. What it means is that any of us who have power tend to use it for our own advantage. This means not only isolated individuals, but we as a political group, as an economic or social class. We use whatever advantages and influence we have to serve our own interests. And there is no exception to this rule. Some of us would like to add "except by the grace of God." But even here the evidence is not clear. Certainly the history of the use of power in the churches tends to support the maxim.

A particularly touching comment on this truth comes out of the early explorations in the New World. Alexander von Humboldt was a scientist and explorer of our early American wilderness. He observed, "In this paradise of the American forests, as well as elsewhere, experience has taught all beings that benignity is seldom found together with power." Lewis Mumford, who cites this quotation, adds, "That statement has universal application."[6] It does indeed. Our treatment of the American Indians is just one ugly example of the truth that power corrupts.

The corrupting effect may be more subtle than savage. I think much of our unconscious racism may be of this kind.

Ours is a white society, and we who have white skins are "in" just by virtue of our color. Most of us quite fail to realize that a person who is black is, by that very fact, an outsider who has to work his way in by some means. In conversations with black friends, I have been made painfully aware of this fact. Ordinarily, we are not sensitive to it. Ethnic groups are trying to make us aware of it, and we resist the truth.

The fact is that we have certain power, certain access to benefits, just by virtue of being white. Without realizing it, we use this power to exclude those who are different—whether blacks or Indians. Sometimes, of course, we use this power openly and violently to exclude minority groups. But many of us who would repudiate open racism are insensitive to the implicit racism which permeates our attitudes and many structures of society.

Why should it be so difficult for blacks to get quality education for their children? Why do they have to fight to be allowed to live in any section of the metropolitan area? It's because we who really control the system are using our control in what seems to be our own interests. Outsiders find it difficult to get in. It is a case of the subtle pervasive corrupting influence of power.

Social scientists have invented a name for such social realities. They call them "cruelty systems." I take this to mean social structures or ways of operating which really oppress or exploit people, whether those in the establishment realize it or not.

This reminds me of some of the current discussions concerning violence. Some social scientists are saying that the power exerted to maintain such structures or systems is really a form of violence—violence against the people who are exploited or suffer discrimination. Violence is not only the use of power to overthrow a system; it is also the use of power to maintain a system which is oppressive or discriminatory. Some spokesmen would conclude from this that it is justifiable for the oppressed to use violence to throw off the power which holds them down. I can see justification for this—as a last resort. But I cannot escape the force of the argument that violence only begets violence. The violence of revolt will arouse the violence of repression.

But if the cruelty systems represent a sort of violence, they also beget violence—the violence of revolt. What we need is the acknowledgment that we who are the establishment may very well be using the implicit power of our position in a way unfavorable to those who are not part of the establishment. It is not easy to become sensitized to this. On the one hand, having power is deceitful; it flatters us that our motives are noble. On the other hand, we want to believe this about ourselves, that we can manage power well.

If the present system is serving us well, we are likely to see no need for change. So we use the power implicit in our position to maintain the status quo, or to limit concessions which have to be made, or to turn change to our own advantage. This is what I hear the critics of our system saying. The haunting question is whether we are open to change without violent reaction against an unresponsive system.

The lesson we all have to learn is that there are no exceptions to the maxim that power corrupts, not even ourselves. It is a popular illusion that we, whoever "we" may be, can be trusted to use power wisely and well. It is the error of every ideology, including popular democracy, to believe that once our side gets into power, everything will be fine. We think of ourselves as trustworthy, and our opponents as unworthy of being given power. We really must disabuse ourselves of this illusion.

I first came across this fallacy in my early studies of Marxism. It seemed very clear there: all the devils were on one side. The state would wither away just as soon as the right people came into power. The right people, of course, could be trusted to rule justly. The illusion was obvious.

But then I realized that the same fallacy pervades our popular democratic thought. If we can just get the power into the right hands, we assume, everything will be solved. "Power to the People!" is a battle cry. But "the People" can't be counted on any more than their antagonists, who are also people.

The simple fact is that nobody can be trusted with too much power. If we all are motivated by self-interest, however enlightened, it follows that we will use whatever power we have for our own advantage. If we can hope to be moved by better motives than that, we still have to be on guard against the subtle deceit which power brings with it. When we have power, it is terrifyingly easy to assure ourselves that we are using it benevolently and wisely.

That's why we need countervailing powers. Whatever power "we" have must be balanced by the power "they" have. Vested interest is set over against another vested interest. Somewhere in here "the public interest" must also be vested with enough power to avoid getting crushed in the conflict. In a democracy we dare to hope that the balancing of rival interests and powers will work toward the greater good of everyone involved. Our hope may be entirely too facile, because there are other factors involved.

## The limits of politics

Every group concerned with social issues looks to political means to realize its goals. The Christian minority will be no different from others in this regard. But rather than constituting a well-defined pressure group, Christians are likely to be scattered among various organizations with whom they identify. Knowing the necessity of political action, we will engage with these allies in activities appropriate to our common goals. However, many of us will do this with a sort of realistic reserve. We know our inclination to abuse power, and suspect this is a universal ailment. Moreover, we are aware of the limits of politics.

Here is another popular belief from which we really need to be delivered. This is the common expectation that we can solve our most serious problems by politics, or by some combination of politics and economics. We seem to believe that if we can just find the right political formula to regulate our economy, everyone will have the good life. The politicians make the promises and devise the programs, and the people wait for the dreams to come true or complain when they don't.

The novelist Ross Lockridge, Jr. observed that politics had become the new American religion.[7] As I recall, he was portraying life in the United States back at the time of the Civil War. He depicted a political rally, complete with parade, bands, oratory, and frenzied crowds, and commented that this was America's new religion. I didn't believe him when I read the novel. I do now. Everything I've seen in American life since that time documents his observation. We expect salvation by political-economic programs.

We must learn to acknowledge the limits of politics. Only politics and economics can solve political and economic problems. But economics and politics alone cannot solve any fundamental human issue. We are living in a time when social problems are especially prominent and painful. It's easy to fall into the trap of supposing that our deepest human needs are of this sort. But this is a misreading of our human condition. Once we see the further reaches of our needs, we recognize that politics and economics really can't help us at these points.

Whenever I think about this particular issue, I am reminded of a line from T. S. Eliot, in which he says that we are "dreaming of systems so perfect that no one will need to be good." And he adds,

> "But the man that is will shadow
> The man that pretends to be."[8]

That's why we need something more than political and economic programs: our human needs and problems are of a more profound and desperate kind.

The first limit of politics is that it cannot, by itself, supply the values and goals of political action. To what ends should we apply political power? What are the goals of economic power? These questions are not answered by politics and economics themselves, but by philosophy and religion.

Irving Babbitt was one of the wisest American thinkers I ever encountered. He stated the case this way a quarter century ago: "When studied with any degree of thoroughness, the economic problem will be found to run into the political problem, the political problem in turn into the philosophical problem, and the philosophical problem itself to be almost indissolubly bound up at last with the religious problem."

Just a few years ago, Daniel Moynihan, addressing a student audience, commented on the limits of politics: "What is it government cannot provide? It cannot provide values to persons who have none, or who have lost those they had. It cannot provide a meaning of life. It cannot provide inner peace. It can provide outlets for moral energies, but it cannot create those energies. In particular, government cannot cope with the crisis in values which is sweeping the Western World."[9] I don't know that it can be said any better than that.

A second limit of politics, hinted at in the preceding quotation, is that it cannot provide the motivation for political action. We human beings are strangely mixed creatures (I don't have to argue that any further). We need some motive more powerful than self-interest to drive us to disinterested political action. We need some powerful concern to enable us to move beyond, perhaps even contrary to, our vested interests in economic action. The American philosopher William Ernest Hocking has said it well: "The state depends for its vitality upon a motivation which it cannot by itself command."[10]

We need a faith which will constrain our lust for power and will release our capacity to care about others. Let's see if we can find one.

## Liberty and justice

If I understand the critiques of such men as Marcuse and Reich, it is their judgment that by the collusion of power in the United States, the freedom of the average citizen is severely limited, perhaps denied. The Corporate State, they charge, gives the illusion of allowing freedom of choice, but the state itself determines what are the alternatives among which we may choose. So the freedom is illusory, unreal; its limits are predetermined by those who control economic and political power.

Whether the critique is wholly accurate or not, the thrust of the positive truth is surely accurate. If there is to be any real liberty, there has to be a balancing of rival powers. The simplest definition of justice is "to each his due." If everyone is to realize this goal, there must be a rough balance of powers. That is, you should not have the kind of power that can prevent me from receiving my due; nor vice versa. And there should be no combine of powers that can inhibit both of us from gaining what is our due.

The ideal of balance is the Greek ideal. For the Greeks, justice in the state meant the proper balance of all its functions and powers. The just state, indeed, was the social counterpart of the just person, in whom all the virtues are well balanced. Nothing too much was the Greek ideal.

Moreover, the Greeks saw that if the state is to achieve justice, it must be governed by people who are just. So the rulers, in Plato's ideal state, are the philosopher-kings, men who are both wise and good. Those who have power must be persons of integrity and goodwill. If we are to be trusted with power, we must have gained personal stability and character. In a democracy this applies to all of us, because political power is shared by the citizens. If Demos is king, Everyman must be noble.

The Hebrew put it in a distinctively different manner. He saw justice as the demand of God, and the achievement of justice as the fruit of obedience to God. It was the prophets who articulated this most clearly. If idolatry was the primal sin, injustice was its most grievous consequence. They affirmed that God requires his people to live together in justice. But they saw that the public disobeyed the command: rulers oppressed the people; those with economic power exploited them; and the people sought solace in sensual indulgences. The achievement of justice required a return to the obedience of God.

The religious dimension of the use of power is beautifully affirmed in the last words of David: "He that ruleth over men must be just, ruling in the fear of God" (II Sam. 23:3 KJV).

If men are to rule in the fear of God, those who challenge the power of the ruler must do so in the same reverence. A comment about the Puritans, attributed I believe to Macauley, illustrates this side of the thesis: "They put their foot in the neck of their king, but they bowed the knee before God."

Again here is an insight which seems almost totally lost today. We have lots of people who are ready to challenge authority, but who do not themselves recognize any higher authority. But all power, including force used against authority, must be exercised in allegiance to a higher loyalty, an ultimate authority. "Under God" is the posture in which we are most likely to find the greatest measure of justice.

The familiar prophetic vision of a world at peace (as in Isaiah 2:1-5) is grounded in such a religious understanding. Although often interpreted as a humanistic hope, it is not that at all. The day when "they shall beat their swords into plowshares, and their spears into pruning hooks" follows upon the acknowledgment of a common religious faith. It is when "the mountain of the house of the Lord shall be established . . ., and all the nations shall flow to it" that there shall be the possibility of peace. It is when people shall say, "Come, let us go up to the mountain of the Lord, to the house of the God of Jacob," that they will follow the ways of justice. Peace and justice are the fruits of the honest worship of God.

## The politics of love

The Christian imperative is really an extension of the Hebrew command. When Jesus said that the second great commandment is to love our neighbors, he was quoting Hebrew scriptures. He quoted this law in order to emphasize it. He underscored it by telling the story of an "outsider" who responded generously to a fellow human being who had been beaten and robbed and abandoned (Luke 10:25-37). He told a story in which the destiny of the characters depended on their response to people hurt by the ills of society (Matthew 25:31-46). So we live under this imperative to care honestly about the well-being of our fellow humans. There is nothing distinctively Christian about this ideal: it is Hebrew; one might even say, it is just plain human. The special Christian insight has to do with Christ himself and what he can do to help us become such a caring person. Still it is true that the imperative to love our neighbor is not exclusively Christian. Which leads me to consider the politics of love on the broadest possible basis.

It's easy to wax sentimental about love. But in talking about social issues we should avoid sentimentality like the plague. Considering the many meanings attached to the term, love may not even be the best word to use. What does it mean?

In the present context love means caring, goodwill, honest concern for others. To love means to be concerned for the good of other human beings, concerned enough to do what may be necessary to realize their well-being. To love others means really to care about what happens to them, and to let your behavior be determined by such caring. To love your neighbor means to do what is necessary to alleviate his pressing needs. But it means also to help build a society which guarantees him opportunity and assures him power to fulfill his basic human needs.

The realization of the ideal of justice requires the motivation of love. It was Reinhold Niebuhr who taught many of our generation this lesson. The motive of love works in two ways. First, it acts as a restraint on my tendency to use selfishly what power I may have. Love makes me sensitive to the circumstances and feelings of my fellow humans, sensitive to the subtle abuse of power to which I am susceptible.

Second, love is the only motive powerful enough to impel me really to seek the good of other people. Self-interest, enlightened though it may be, simply is not a strong enough motive to compel me to risk personal vested interests for your sake, especially if "you" are a stranger, or "different," or distant. Moreover, if we all are operating from self-interest, we really have no basis for trusting one another. The best we can hope for is an uneasy truce, a cautious alliance. And this is no solid justice.

Justice requires love for its motivation. Power needs love for its constraint and direction. But love needs power, in order to realize its goals. Justice is usually the best that love can manage to achieve. Love, in this sense, must be politicized. If politics needs love as motive, love needs politics as method.

"Make love, not war" is a slogan which some rebellious youth used to flaunt. It may be a better maxim than they—or those who were offended by it—realized. Is it possible for us to build a social order which, rather than inciting us to violence, will encourage us to care about one another? The question is rhetorical but very real. Frankly, I'm not sure of the answer. What I am sure of is that the pressure is on us to become people who really care about what happens to people. It may be here that the Christian message has a relevant word to offer.

We really need help in becoming people who care. What gets in the way of our love is all the mixed-up feelings and attitudes we have been talking about. Our self-will, our sense of alienation, our fears and hostilities, our pride and false ambition—we need a cleaning job, and a remodeling.

The Christian faith says that this is available. God has made the offer in Jesus Christ. We can start becoming this kind of caring person—now, if we will. Then what we need is the continuing process of learning and growing, becoming aware and sensitive. Then comes the long, tiresome, frequently discouraging job of trying to get the system to respond to the neglected needs of segments of society. In fact, this job won't wait until we have enough caring people around. We have to get done what is possible and keep trying to do what seems impossible. We have to be working at all these things at the same time.

It's all right to be "innocent as doves." But it is suggested that we should also be "wise as serpents." A love that is harmless won't get much done. We require the best of political wisdom and cleverness to accomplish love's goals. We must have love to keep us from using our cleverness simply for our own advantage. Love needs power; power needs love.

# VII. Craft Idiocy and Work Ethic
## (By the sweat of whose brow?)

> In his insistence on the importance of the spirit of
> work Luther antedated Marx. ... He considered
> one craft as good a way to personal perfection as
> another; but also as bad a potential lifelong prison
> as another.
>
> —Erik Erikson[1]

"The mass of men lead lives of quiet desperation. ... A stereotyped but unconscious despair is concealed even under what are called the games and amusements of mankind."[2] This striking observation was written more than a century ago, in quiet, bucolic New England! Can anyone deny its relevance to our condition today?

I would like to stake out the claim that much of our despair is rooted in our confused understanding of the meaning of work, our inadequate goals and purposes for work, a feeling of senseless accomplishment in our work. Because we don't know what "work" means, we don't even know how to "play."

The very word "work" arouses all sorts of confused reactions among us.

One popular notion is that work is something for us to avoid, if we can; we try to get away with doing as little as possible.

Or it is grudgingly accepted as an economic necessity.

It may even be thought of as a moral value, the earnest practice of which will yield proper rewards.

So work may become a compulsive pursuit of monetary and material achievements. Or we feel that if we aren't working, we are wasting time.

"All work and no play makes Jack a dull boy." So we try to escape from meaningless work into equally meaningless play.

Or we sense the emptiness of life without work. Middle-aged men face retirement with apprehension. "What will we do, if we are no longer working?" And their wives worry about having them underfoot. The young, having rejected work as a way of life, find themselves bored, with nothing significant to do.

For the religious, there are faint echoes from dimly remembered narratives. Does the creation story really say that work is a curse? And the commandment: "Six days shalt thou labor. . . ." Man, that's passé. Today we dream of a four-day work week, with three days to tire ourselves out with exhausting play. So much for the inherent rhythm of labor and re-creation.

It isn't easy to find our way among these confusing alternatives. But we must try. Our personal integrity and fulfillment may very well depend on a sense that we are doing something worthwhile with our lives. Our contribution to a healthy civilization may depend on our understanding of what our vocation is. Building a civilization is hard work. This is true in almost any sense of the word used. But we will engage in such work only if we have an adequate appreciation of what it means and our own place in it.

## A working definition

Perhaps what we need first is some sort of definition. It is not easy to define work clearly, but we can try.

To work means to spend your energy, to use your powers, in order to accomplish a chosen purpose. This is a basic definition which I think must be stated clearly, especially in view of our current confusion.

To think of work only as a job, as gainful employment, is really quite inadequate. This may be the most common definition, but it is no less insufficient because of its popularity. To work is not primarily to do a job. It is basically to spend your energy for a purpose. The nature of work depends entirely on the chosen purpose. If you are working in order to make a living—that is, by definition, a job. But if work means exerting your energies, this applies not only to what you do at your machine or in your office. It applies also to what you do around the house: washing dishes or mowing the lawn. Practicing the piano or learning how to throw a curve ball or mastering the art of making buttonholes—this is work.

There's a sense in which play is work. Just because we

do it "for fun," we seldom think of it as work. But "the sweat of the brow" is brought out as much by chasing a basketball up and down the court as it is by hauling garbage cans. Playing tennis may be more fun than pitching hay, but it is no less work. Indeed, I would guess that the professional athlete or entertainer works as hard at his business as the ditch digger or salesman. The amateur may make a sport of it, but the professional isn't playing games. Similarly, the artist works at his art. There are few disciplines more demanding than those of the arts and the professions.

Marcuse takes what seems to be a characteristic Freudian position and distinguishes between work and pleasure. He expresses his hope "to make the human body an instrument of pleasure rather than labor."[3] We can understand why any normal human being would grab hold of such a thesis, especially if he doesn't read any further. Who wouldn't rather have fun than work and have no energy left for play?

But if you read further—which is not always easy with Marcuse; it's frequently hard work—you learn that he takes back what he has so alluringly offered. In a footnote he admits that "not every kind and mode of labor is essentially irreconcilable with the pleasure principle." Or, more directly, "not all work is unpleasurable."[4] In other words, there may be a deep satisfaction to be found in work itself.

This is true, if we have an adequate definition of work. If we know that it means using our powers for purposes we believe worthwhile, then we can see that meaningful work may indeed yield the truest satisfactions we can experience. Work can be fun!

## Work as human need

It is imperative to recognize that, in this basic sense of the word, work is a fundamental human need. I suspect that this is not commonly understood but it must be, for the sake of our personal satisfaction and our cultural recovery. Let me summon a few witnesses who may strengthen the case.

Peter Drucker flatly says, "Work is a psychological and social necessity for man and not only a way to earn our daily bread."[5] He is surely right. And Mumford expresses a similar value judgment when he affirms, "There is no substitute for work except other serious work."[6] Paul Goodman bases his scathing indictment of our society on the underlying conviction that "except in worthwhile activity there is no way to be happy."[7]

A most eloquent paragraph, which seems to bring together both definition of work and recognition of need, is a Marxist's summary of Marx's own understanding of work. William Williams, an influential American historian, writes:

> When Marx says that labor should cease to be "merely a means of life" and become instead "life's principle (sic) need," he is courageously substituting the classical meaning of work for the capitalistic definition of man as a quantum of energy in the marketplace. He is saying that the central need of the individual is to fulfill himself in creative labor which produces relationships which humanize and strengthen and sustain his community with other individuals.[8]

I don't know that it can be said any better. Except that I don't see why it requires any particular "courage" to affirm a "classical meaning of work." All it needs is a certain insight and understanding—which is what I am trying to offer right here.

I believe that Jesus' parable of the talents (Matthew 25:14-30) is relevant to such an interpretation of work. I know the dangers of reading current ideas into the ancient texts. (I have heard this story used as a defense of American Capitalism.) But I know also that continuing aspects of our human condition are reflected in these documents. Here is one such.

Three men are entrusted with varying numbers of talents, which means literally varying amounts of money. Each was given a trust "according to his ability." Each was judged by the use he made of the "talents" lent to him. Those who used their opportunities productively, creatively, were rewarded with still greater responsibilities ("you have been faithful over a little, I will set you over much"). And they won a sense of fulfillment ("enter into the joy of your master"). The one who failed to use his powers was not only rebuked ("you wicked and slothful servant!"), but he lost the very gift with which he had been entrusted.

This parable seems to me to be affirming some fundamental and important truths about ourselves. All of us have creative and productive powers. Obviously, some of us are more gifted than others. But our value as human beings does not depend on how many are our gifts. Each is valued for whatever talent, however limited, he has.

The fulfillment of our existence lies in developing and using our talents (meaning now not sums of money, but abilities, gifts, powers). The real joy of living is to be found in the creative satisfaction of knowing we are making good use of our talents. In fact, I'd be willing to bet that there is no solid satisfaction in life without this sense of meaningful accomplishment. Our frenzied pursuit of excitement is a futile chase after satisfaction where it cannot be found. What we deeply long for is creative fulfillment.

(It occurs to me that this is probably true even in our confused sexual indulgences—perhaps especially here. For the creative significance of sex is undeniable. To use it for merely pleasurable purposes is self-defeating. Isn't it rather remarkable that the most intense personal pleasure is linked with the most miraculous creative process in which we share!)

If you want to be a real person, you must be engaged in some kind of self-fulfilling, other-serving activity. Work is disciplined effort directed toward a desired end. The quality of your life depends on the purpose which you most deeply desire. The satisfaction you experience depends both on the quality of that chosen goal, and your ability to direct your powers toward its achievement.

**The demeaning of work**

One of the most serious indictments of our society is that we have raised a false ideal of work and have failed to provide our people with opportunities for truly meaningful work. The false understandings are generally mixed up with equally false values and goals for our living. So we see work as the means to make a pile of money, at least enough to live as comfortably as our neighbors. Or we think of work as a necessary discomfort to be endured, so as to be able to afford the pleasures we'd like to enjoy. Or we embrace competitiveness as a way of life and assume that the rewards always go to the most deserving. In each instance, we are confronted with not only a shoddy interpretation of work but a cheap valuation of the purpose of existence.

The charge that our society has robbed us of the opportunity for significant work is made most seriously by Paul Goodman in *Growing up Absurd*. The opening sentence of his first chapter is a sharp statement of the issue: "It's hard to grow up when there isn't enough man's work."[9] By "man's work" he means significant employment, working at meaningful tasks. Apart from the evident sexist attitude which he reveals, there is no denying his assertion. He says that our society simply does not offer enough opportunities for meaningful work. As a consequence, many of us are condemned to spend our lives at jobs which offer neither challenge nor fulfillment. He claims that it isn't possible really to "grow up" in such a society. "By and large our economic society is *not* geared for the cultivation of its young or the attainment of important goals that they can work toward." How can a thoughtful person live with this awful fact: "During my productive years I will spend eight hours a day doing what is no good."[10]

Charles Reich offers a similar critique of American society. "The Corporate State . . .," he declares, "is now bringing about its own destruction."[11] It is doing this because it is no longer able to motivate willing workers and willing consumers. If people are going to work hard, they must really want the rewards that are offered. Reich claims that for increasing numbers of our people, the rewards are not worth the effort.

At the heart of this "self-destruction" lies the fact that "American society no longer has any viable concept of work."[12] We are asked to work hard, but are offered only external satisfactions, and they are no longer enough for most of us. Actually, I fear that the consequence is not so much the breakdown of the system—which Reich sees— as it is the demeaning of our own lives.

The result is what Marx has called "craft-idiocy." His concept of "alienated work" is probably better known. That is, we may be condemned to work at jobs which are really foreign to our humanity, and the performance of which simply alienates us from ourselves. This is true enough, I would guess; but I like his phrase "craft idiocy" much better. I came across it in my reading in quite another field.[13] By it Marx seems to mean that most of us simply accept the definition of work which is offered us in our middle-class modified capitalism. We conform to the goals and values held before us, and we find ourselves locked into meaningless jobs which offer us no satisfactions except those which our society defines for us.

"Craft-idiocy," indeed! But how shall we escape from such a box?

The first requirement would seem to be commitment to a more humane understanding of what work means. I have already tried to outline such an interpretation. Now it needs to be extended to the development of a more adequate "work ethic."

## Toward a Christian work ethic

A funny thing happened to the Protestant work ethic on its way to our contemporary economy. It became secularized and therefore no longer Protestant. But few people have been sensitive enough to change its name. This is either dishonest or foolhardy. If you don't care what happens to the word "protestant," you need not feel uneasy about allowing the adjective to be applied to an undesirable attitude, whether it fits or not. In fact, this is a good way to degrade the term, and if you would welcome that, here's a way to do it safely. But if you put any value on the word "protestant," it is foolhardy to let it be used in this way, when what is being identified is no longer authentically Protestant.

I want to protest the secularization of the work ethic in our society and propose a recovery of its truly Christian orientation.

The relation of the Protestant ethic to our capitalistic economy has been the subject of long and informative inquiry. There seems to be a most interesting interaction. What hasn't been called to our attention with equal clarity is that the Protestant ethic itself underwent a serious change. In the development of capitalism, the underlying work ethic was secularized.[14] I contend that a secular ethic is no longer truly Protestant and should not be called by the name.

That is to say, the Protestant ethic is grounded in the Protestant faith. This classic faith has been seriously undermined in our culture during the past two centuries (or even four, depending on how you read history). Gradually, the work ethic was separated from its foundation in faith. The faith diminished, even disappeared. The ethic continued to be affirmed. But such an ethic, without any grounding in faith, is no longer "protestant." It is a secular work ethic and doesn't deserve to be identified with the classic term for a definite theological point of view.

I am ready to admit that the churches, their preachers and teachers, have shared in this decline. Some of my friends can cite chapter and verse, that is, sermon and address, in which Christian spokesmen have orated about the value of hard work, the divine sanctions upon faithful labor, and the assured rewards of diligence. But I don't care who has done it, whether learned academician or should-have-known-better preacher. The result is the same. The secularization of the work ethic tears it from its theological context. It is no longer a Protestant ethic, even when preached from a Protestant pulpit.

While we are trying to clarify our language, we may go all the way and stop using the word "protestant" altogether. What we need, really, is a *Christian* work ethic. There are good historical reasons why this particular subject has been called "protestant." But those circumstances have passed. Now what we need is a broader work ethic, freed from its historical limitations, open to anyone who takes the Christian claim seriously.

This was brought home to me one Sunday morning, after I had discussed the subject in a sermon. A lady shook my hand after the service and said, "I'm a Catholic. Can I join you in this ethic you're talking about? And maybe we can call it a Christian work ethic?"

We can indeed. So from this moment on, let me stop fretting about what has happened to the Protestant aspects of our work ethic. Let me try to outline a doctrine of work that can be called Christian.

The faith in which a Christian work ethic is grounded can be stated in several theses.

1. God's primary work is the work of creation: creating and sustaining a good world for the good of his creatures.

2. However, we human beings have tossed a wrench into the machinery; we have thrown everything out of gear, including ourselves.

3. Consequently, our deepest need is to be "put right," within ourselves, with God, in relation to reality.

4. God's second and continuing work, then, is what is called "redemption," making it possible for us to be authentically related to the whole of reality.

If I understand the history of the West, this faith has long since been discarded by most intellectuals and disregarded by most of the rest of us. In fact, I suspect that many preachers and church members no longer take this faith seriously. I want to repeat that, without it, there can be no Christian ethic.

But to return to our present task, let me summarize the work ethic which does emerge from the classic Christian faith.

5. When we are set right, we are called to join with God in his work of creation and redemption: to build a humane civilization, to try to overcome the cumulative effects of our folly. (This is called "vocation.")

6. Our abilities, our energies, our time, our financial resources are not ours to do with as we please; they are endowments entrusted to us by God, to be used for his purposes. We are not owners, only trustees or managers. (This is called "stewardship.")

7. Some practical virtues which grow out of this view are: willingness to work hard; pride in working well; trustworthiness; concern for one another.

There it is, and we must keep it all together. If we don't, all kinds of serious errors occur. To knock yourself out trying to make a pile of money is not the Protestant ethic, although it seems often to be identified as such. Nor is the common attitude of valuing a person by the size of his income. To exploit a fellow human being in the name of profit or competition cannot be justified by any kind of ethic, let alone Christian. Every one of these instances is a cruel violation of Christian faith, therefore of the Christian ethic.

The Christian work ethic is to engage with God in his work in the world. This is where the Christian minority will be found, scattered throughout the secular jobs in society, finding ways and occasions of doing God's work: trying to eliminate exploitation and discrimination;

seeking the political and economic means of realizing human goals; working for a social order that will guarantee opportunities to all; trying to clarify values and goals for our common life; injecting Christian meanings into the business of making a living; and working at these tasks, working hard and gladly, because caught up in a purpose which is greater than anything we can devise, a purpose which we believe to be God's will.

After having said all this, I must still put in a good word for a secular form of this work ethic. Even if you do remove the faith, there is still a valid secular residue in the ethic. It seems to me that, if we are to build a viable society, we must have people who are willing to work hard, who take pride in working well, who can be trusted in their dealings, and who have a genuine concern for other people. Christianity to one side, these human values are fundamental to society.

It's rather like the Ten Commandments. They don't constitute a Christian ethic, but society can't get along without them. Incidentally, when was the last time anyone noticed that the first four commandments deal not with social behavior but with our attitude toward God? Maybe this says something to us. In fact, it says just what I am trying to say about a work ethic.

The ethic does not—cannot—stand alone. The ethic has validity only when it is affirmed in a context of faith. The ethic has power to direct our behavior only when it is driven by the motive of a larger, deeper faith.

That's another reason why we must keep it all together.

## The doctrine of vocation

On the basis of such a faith and ethic, we can reconstruct another classic Protestant doctrine which has larger Christian significance: the doctrine of vocation. Simply stated, this affirms that every Christian person is called by God to help him do his work in the world. Whatever our daily job may be, it can be an opportunity to serve God and our fellow human beings. (Of course, there are some jobs which can hardly be interpreted as service to God and our fellows. It seems to me that Christians will avoid such employment, if it is humanly possible. If not, we believe God takes such factors into consideration.) Every task, no matter how humble or seemingly insignificant, can be important in his sight.

This truth figured in Luther's understanding of the Christian life, which is why it has been known historically as Protestant. I find it significant that Erikson, in his study of the Reformer, interprets this doctrine so wisely. He comments, "Luther was against works, but very much for work; . . . he sanctified even such activities as piling up manure, washing babies, and cleaning up the house, if they were done with faith."[15]

There are two sides to this incisive truth. If it is true that any useful work can be a way of serving God, it is also true that there may be some jobs which God does not want us to do. If "one craft [is] as good a way to personal perfection as another," it is also true that a particular craft may be "as bad a potential lifelong prison as another." Erikson states it very wisely: "Many individuals should not do the work which they are doing, if they are doing it well at too great inner expense. . . . The point is, not how efficiently the work is done, but how good it is for the worker."[16]

So, to the extent it is open to us, we must choose our vocations in consideration of our own capacities, broad human needs, and our insight into the divine will. Profit and personal advantage are never sufficient motives for Christian vocational decision. God may want us to serve some human need, even at personal "disadvantage." The reward will have to be of his own devising.

God has his work to do in the world—to sustain human values, to redeem human error, to combat destructive forces. But he can't do his work without us. He has only human hands and hearts, only human words and deeds, only human structures and systems, by which to get his will done. If God's will is to be done on earth in any measure at all, it will be done only as we humans do it.

Do we believe that God wills a just political order? If so, who's going to do it? The politicians—and those who elect them. That is to say, Christian politicians are called to do God's work in the political order, and Christian citizens to support them there.

Do we believe that God wills an equitable economic system? If so, who's going to do this? Businessmen, and all who work with them. So we may say that Christian businessmen, laborers and their leaders, executives and managers, owners and stockholders—all are called of God to serve him in the economic order.

This is true throughout every necessary and helpful

task in the whole range of society. Every one of us is called; it is our vocation to serve God in our daily work. And not only in our employment, but also in every place of responsibility and service which is open to us: In community organizations and political parties, in schools and school boards, in professions and professional societies, in churches and church-related projects, in home and family. The list is as endless as the tasks to be done in society. You can add opportunities which come to your mind.

Do you dare believe that what you do where you are, day in and day out, is your vocation, God's call for you to serve him? Such a faith will have its effect on your vocational and avocational decisions. If you haven't yet made your vocational choice, this faith will surely put pressure on you to move in useful directions. If you are already committed to a vocation, you must be able to conceive of it as doing God's work in the world. If for any reason you can't say this, and can't get out of what you are doing, then you must find opportunities for such service in your avocational opportunities.

The reward? The sheer joy of knowing that you are engaged with God in his service. There may also be personal growth and larger opportunity ("you have been faithful over a little, I will set you over much"). Realistically, these developments may not be so obvious and may never amount to what you might hope. But I believe such a commitment to vocation will yield an increasing sense of fulfillment and enjoyment: The quiet excitement of knowing that what you are doing really does matter—if to no one else, certainly to God, and if to him, then also to others; the creative satisfaction of knowing that you are making productive use of whatever talents you have —and if your gifts are modest, that's not what concerns God, only how you use them.

"Enter into the joy of your master."

# VIII. Hope Springs Eternal
## (But how can you tell it from illusion?)

> The new Jerusalem is to be established at the end of time, but absolutely not by any human effort. She is a creation of God, and her nature, therefore, is the opposite of a golden age. Instead of being the continuation of history, the crowning act of history is a break with history. The second creation stands over against the first, which it is impossible to draw back from destruction. ... Let there be no confusion: there is no use expecting a new Jerusalem on earth. Jerusalem will be God's creation, absolutely free, unforeseeable, transcendent. But God's act gives man room for autonomous action.
>
> —Jacques Ellul[1]

We are creatures of hope. We cling to hope when all the evidence is against us. The poet's comment is certainly true: "Hope springs eternal in the human breast." I don't like the second line so much: "Man never is, but always to be, blest." That isn't altogether true. We are in fact blessed in many ways, but never quite so much as we expect. So we hope for something better.

Is our hope simply wishful thinking? Are we trying to cushion the shock of hard reality? It would be unwise to deny that some hopes are probably expressions of an unwillingness to face reality. But there is evidence that something deeper is involved also.

So Erik Erikson writes that hope is one of the essential human strengths we need in order to live effectively. "Hope is both the earliest and the most indispensable virtue inherent in the state of being alive."[2] By "virtue" he means a strength for living. Such strengths must be gained at the different stages of personal development. And hope is "the first and most basic and yet it is also the most lasting" of these strengths.[3] As hope matures it becomes faith, and religion supplies a "world-image" to sustain it.

Still we realize that hope must be authentic. There must be something in reality corresponding to it, or at least supporting it. We can't go on deceiving ourselves, living by illusions. So we must ask what is real.

**Hope and illusion**

Our capacity for hope is rooted in reality. Our need for hope reflects reality. Let's test these statements.

Our capacity for hope is a mark of our origin. We know instinctively that we have been called into being by a power greater than ourselves—if nothing else, the cosmos itself. Our existence is shaped by the purposes of a Creator who is the source of all life. Hope is the forward look of this remembered intuition: it is the anticipation that the purposes implicit in our being will finally be realized, that the potentials given us will open out into fulfillment. Our origin cannot be denied. It looks toward a destiny.

Our need for hope is grounded in our sense that we were intended for a destiny greater than anything we have yet known or achieved. Our intended destiny is the fulfillment of our origin. God has made us for purposes which we frustrate and even defy. Yet these purposes are ultimately undeniable. Their deep presence in our being stimulates a hopefulness that cannot be entirely repressed. We were made for something far better than we have ever managed to realize. The implicit knowledge of this truth is the ground of hope. Our being longs for fulfillment. So we need to hope.

Unfortunately, what happens to hope is exactly what happens to every other gift granted us. We misread its intent. We tear it loose from its true purpose. We reshape it in an image of our own devising. We use it for our own purposes. The gift is spoiled—whether feeling or will or reason or hope. It becomes something else—rebelliousness or alienation or pride or illusion. When we distort our proper relation with God, everything in life is thrown into disarray.

The same thing happens to hope. Because we cannot live without hope of some kind, we devise false hopes. Hope becomes illusion. But we don't know the difference, because we have lost sight of the original intent. The need for hope persists. So we feed it with illusions and wonder why we are so frequently disillusioned. We wonder why our hopes seem empty even when realized—perhaps especially when realized. We hope for something. Then when we get it, we say, "Why did I ever want that!" Then off we go, chasing another illusion.

I take it to be a primary task of Christian faith to unmask illusion and point to authentic hope. This is often a thankless job, because it destroys so many favorite idols. It is also painful, because we like to cling to our little securities. But the task must first be destructive before it can be constructive. Illusions must be identified for what they are, in order to make way for authentic hope. We must learn to live without illusion, so that we may live with hope.

## Immortality and resurrection

One illusion from which we need to be delivered is the popular notion of immortality. It is probably a safe guess that most people believe that every human being has an immortal soul. This soul, they believe, will be released after the death of the body into some kind of eternal life. Then, it is commonly assumed, everything will probably turn out fine for everybody.

There are variations on this last theme, of course. Some tough-minded Christians believe that most people —all except the true believers—will be consigned to eternal punishment. Some gentler persons reserve such a fate for the few really horrible criminals who have been produced in history—and there may be some question even about them. But most people simply assume that

130    *Christian Counter Culture*

everything will turn out all right, and a good-natured deity will see that all souls reach whatever heaven is.

What we have to get at is the basic belief in immortality. This is not a biblical teaching but a Greek idea which has persisted in Western thought. Actually, the belief that humans are endowed with immortal souls was baptized into the church. This was really unfortunate, because it has resulted in a lot of inadequate notions which pass for Christian orthodoxy.

Actually, almost all reputable biblical scholars recognize that neither the Old nor the New Testament teaches that we human beings have immortal souls as part of our native endowment. What the New Testament affirms is not immortality but resurrection.[4] This is an important distinction which must be made, if we are to be intelligently faithful to the New Testament. Our Christian hope is not that we have immortal souls that will live forever. Our hope is that the God whom we love and serve will raise us to a new dimension of life in his eternal Kingdom. Eternal life is not a native human endowment. It is the gift of God. Our proper hope is that, if we give our lives to God's purposes here and now, he will find a place for us to continue to serve him in eternity.

There are a good many issues involved in this whole question, especially as they relate to our destiny as persons. Let me simply say that I understand this faith to be the hope that we shall be raised to a new kind of life, life in a quite different dimension. We will be given new bodies adequate to the heightened quality of life in this new world. It will be an existence characterized by con-

*Hope Springs Eternal*     131

tinuing service and growth. It will be the ultimate fulfillment of the purposes for which we were made. Our humanity will be fully realized in the life of God's eternal Kingdom. This is the hope by which we live.

## Utopia and the kingdom of God

There is another popular illusion from which we suffer: utopianism. Styles of utopianism are varied. They may run from a highly sophisticated belief to a very naïve assumption. But they all come down to the same thing: confidence that somehow, sometime, the human race will succeed in solving its problems and establishing a peaceful, happy world.

The usual hope is that, by some combination of political acumen and technological development, we will resolve the serious problems of war and poverty and racism. This is generally mixed with a naïve belief in progress: we certainly have progressed from where the race was, well, some centuries ago. (This, of course, is true in many important ways.) So the expectation is projected that such progress will continue and be extended to all human problems. The prophetic vision of a world united in peace by a common faith is secularized to a humanistic hope for a pluralistic assembly of people who agree to live and let live. Sometimes, however, this hope is graced with a religious commitment that sees such a utopia as God's will for mankind.

I have to say that in my judgment this is an illusion. And, when advocated in the name of Christianity, it is a

132    *Christian Counter Culture*

misreading of the New Testament. I see nothing in this collection of writings that encourages me to believe that God guarantees that we human beings will finally manage to build a peaceful, just world. Indeed, as I read these documents, the movement of history seems destined to go in quite another direction, until some great cataclysm brings it all to a crashing halt. However we may interpret the blazing symbols of this denouement, I see no way of making them mean inevitable progress to a historical utopia.

In a recent conference which I attended, a most earnest young man burst out impatiently, "I hate to see Christians surrendering their utopianism." I tried to suggest that, as I understand the meaning of the words, Christianity has never really been utopian.

I agree entirely with Northrop Frye, who concludes a brief study of utopia with this judgment: "A Christian utopia, in the sense of an ideal state to be attained in human life, is impossible."[5] He strengthens his argument with an observation about Sir Thomas More, who invented the very word utopia. More was certainly a devout Christian, but the ideal state which he portrays is not really Christian. It is a state in which the "natural virtues" (justice, temperance, fortitude, prudence) are realized, and it turns out to be a much better place than anything Christendom has produced!

Our hope for history really is much more modest than any utopian view. Utopianism can only lead to self-deception or disillusionment. We would do better to be more realistic about what we expect to achieve in history. Our hope is that we may find what Reinhold Niebuhr calls "proximate solutions for insoluble problems." And he adds that "our knowledge that there is no complete solution for the problem would save us from resting in some proximate solution under the illusion that it is an ultimate one."[6]

The Christian hope looks beyond history. I am squarely with the French social scientist, Jacques Ellul, at this point. His language may be sharp and his judgments unyielding. But I believe he reads the New Testament accurately: the "new Jerusalem" is God's creation, not achieved by human effort but introduced by divine decision, not the continuation of history but a kingdom beyond history.[7]

So the author of Revelation envisions "a new heaven and a new earth; for the first heaven and the first earth had passed away." He sees "the holy city, new Jerusalem, coming down out of heaven from God" (Rev. 21:1-4). Symbolic language? To be sure. But hardly symbolizing a historical achievement by human development. Whatever it is, it appears to be God's doing, and beyond history.

In an extraordinary, almost ecstatic vision, Paul sees the movement toward this fulfillment as a vast cosmic process. The present order, our way of doing things, is a living toward death. But this is not the divine intention for the cosmos. Indeed, it is as if creation were in childbirth, groaning toward its fulfillment, a release from death and all the death-dealing forces which threaten our humanity. The cosmos is yearning toward liberation, lib-

eration from the hostilities and estrangements and mis-
directions which are spoiling not only human society but
the earth itself. It is our hope that God will bring about
that release. (Romans 8:18-25.) The "new heaven and
new earth" of John's revelation constitute the liberated
cosmos of Paul's vision.

Both John and Paul affirm that we can be caught up in
this process. We can participate in the fulfillment of the
divine purpose. Our lives can be instruments for the im-
plementing of God's will. By yielding ourselves to his
purposes here and now, we can be carried beyond history
into the cosmic fullness of his will. Because this outcome
looks beyond history, it cannot be defeated by anything
that happens in history. So we live in a hope which need
not be defeated, which indeed can "overcome the
world."

## Here and now

Such a hope helps nerve us for the work we have to do
here and now. At first sight this may not seem to be the
case. So we have to look a little more carefully.

We have tried to be realistic at every point of the argument. We are a minority and probably always will be. We
are discontent with our present culture but also with any
visible alternative. So we join forces with any group that
shares some common goals with us and does not deny
our basic beliefs. We try to inject our peculiar vision into
whatever serious thinking is done. We point to a dimension of reality not commonly considered. Hopefully,

such efforts will improve the quality of social action: we ourselves become more effective persons, and we may help build more adequate social structures.

But now we are saying that we don't really expect to achieve a problem-free society, that the kingdom of God isn't likely to come on earth as it is in heaven (as the Lord's Prayer is so often misstated). What then? Doesn't this final bit of so-called realism cut the nerve of responsible action in society? My answer is a resounding negative followed by an equally resounding affirmation. Such forthright realism strengthens the deepest motivation of our social concern.

It is easy to conclude that, if we can't expect to build a brave new world, we really don't have much reason to knock ourselves out trying to improve matters. Why bother, we may say; we can't win anyway. But this is a misreading of two facts: the real motive for Christian concern and the true implication of honest hope.

The real motivation for Christian social action is not hope but love. We want to build a better society, because we really care about the people who are being hurt by the present system. Actually, if we expect too much, we are going to be disillusioned anyway. And disillusionment really does cut the nerve of patient, unsurrendering effort.

If our hope is realistic, we will be driven to social concern by our honest caring about our fellow human beings. The knowledge that there are no permanent solutions doesn't keep us from seeking what Niebuhr calls "proximate solutions." And our concern for others, especially those who are getting hurt, keeps us working continually at the never-finished task of moving from one "solution" to the next.

Our hope, we have said, looks well beyond these temporary reactions to temporal problems. Yet it has its own powerful effect on our efforts in time. We believe deeply that the eternal purposes of God will not be defeated, that the divine intentions which are engraved in our being will be realized. This assurance gives us courage and patience to persist in our commitment to his purposes as we understand them in history. Such a hope releases an extraordinary power to overcome the hindrances and opposition that we will surely encounter.

I am greatly indebted to a friend who recently reminded me of a passage in Paul's letter to the Romans (5:1-5) which seems to pull together much that I have tried to articulate in these chapters. Let me try to paraphrase the passage.

Our rebelliousness is forgiven and our alienation healed ("justified," "we have peace"). So we "stand in grace"; we experience acceptance and reconciliation. Our hope, then, is that we are living toward the destiny for which God has made us. We hope to recover "the glory of God," which is precisely the "glory" which we have spoiled by our self-willed foolishness (cf. Rom. 3:23).

This hope confirms itself to us in our experience. We suffer all the confusions and hurts which are our common human lot. But such experiences, lived through patiently, produce a strength which gives courage to hope. And this hope never lets us down, because it is grounded in our authentic experience of the love and power of God himself.

"Such a hope is no mockery" (Rom. 5:5 NEB). This hope is indeed no illusion. It is the reflection of reality. Such a hope is rooted in our origin in the creative purpose of God. It looks to the destiny for which God has made us, and confirms itself to us in the present reality of experience. We "stand in" a grace which renews the divine image within us and shapes our relations with others. This authentic hope is at once a vision of eternity and a present strength.

# Notes

## Chapter I

1 Reinhold Niebuhr, *The Children of Light and the Children of Darkness* (New York: Charles Scribner's Sons, 1944), p.17.
2 Lewis Mumford, *The Pentagon of Power* (New York: Harcourt Brace Jovanovich, 1970), p. 432.
3 Herbert Marcuse, *Eros and Civilisation* (London: Sphere Books, 1969), p. 13.
4 Charles Reich, *The Greening of America* (New York: Random House, 1970), pp. 354, 381-82.
5 The concluding words of Theodore Roszak, *The Making of a Counter Culture* (Anchor Books; Garden City, N.Y.: Doubleday & Co., 1969), p. 268.
6 *The Pentagon of Power,* Preface and p. 435.
7 Mark Gerzon, *The Whole World Is Watching* (New York: Viking Press, 1969), p. 220.
8 Reinhold Niebuhr, *The Children of Light and the Children of Darkness,* p. 17.

## Chapter II

1 *The Whole World Is Watching,* p. 130.
2 Cf. Herbert Marcuse, *Eros and Civilisation,* Chapter 3, pp. 59-74.
3 Cf. Norman O. Brown, one of the most popular of the current interpreters of Freud: "Freud's myth of the rebellion of the sons

against the father in the primal, prehistoric horde is not a historical explanation of origins, but a supra-historical archetype; eternally recurrent; a myth; an old, old story." *Love's Body* (New York: Random House, 1972; Paperback Ed.), p. 3.

4 *The Whole World Is Watching*, p. 130.

5 Cf. Erik Erikson, *Identity: Youth and Crisis* (New York: W. W. Norton & Co., 1958), pp. 29-30.

6 *The Making of a Counter Culture*, p. 13.

7 An exclamation of Heidegger, quoted by R. D. Laing, *The Politics of Experience* (Penguin Books; England: Harmondsworth, 1967), p. 46.

## Chapter III

1 *The Politics of Experience*, Introduction, pp. 11, 12.

2 *The Making of a Counter Culture*, p. 232, and p. 95.

3 Erik Erikson, *Insight and Responsibility* (New York: W. W. Norton & Co., 1964), pp. 153-54. Cf. also pp. 101-2. Estrangement, he says, is "ontogenetic," that is, an integral part of our development and growth (p. 104).

4 *The Politics of Experience*, pp. 11, 12.

5 Such a study as *American Violence*, edited by Richard Hofstadter and Michael Wallace (New York: Alfred A. Knopf, 1970), is unpleasantly convincing.

6 *The Pentagon of Power*, pp. 18-19.

7 *Touch the Earth*, compiled by T. C. McLuhan (New York: Outerbridge & Dienstfrey, 1971), p. 73.

8 John Rechy, *City of Night* (Panther Books; London: Hamilton & Co. [Stafford], 1970), pp. 115, 359.

9 The title of Chapter 1 of B. F. Skinner, *Beyond Freedom and Dignity* (New York: Alfred A. Knopf, 1971).

10 Cf. his parables of the lost sheep, coin, and son, Luke 15; and the dramatic account of his seeking out Zacchaeus, Luke 19: 1-10.

## Chapter IV

1 *The Making of a Counter Culture*, pp. 50-51.

2 *Time*, March 13, 1972, p. 51.

3 *IEEE* Spectrum, January, 1972, p. 52.

4 *Identity: Youth and Crisis,* p. 314.

5 E.g., William Ernest Hocking, in *The Coming World Civilization* (New York: Harper & Brothers, 1956); Arthur Koestler, in *The Lotus and the Robot* (New York: Harper & Row, 1971).

6 Mark Gerzon, *The Whole World Is Watching,* p. 223.

7 See esp. Chapter VIII of *The Making of a Counter Culture.*

8 *Ibid.,* p. 258.


## An Interlude:

1 Cf. C. A. Pennington, *With Good Reason* (Nashville: Abingdon Press, 1967), p. 65.

2 Graham Greene in *The End of the Affair* (New York: Viking Press, 1961). Cf. C. A. Pennington, *Liberated Love* (Philadelphia: Pilgrim Press, 1972).

3 See the amazing Chapter 15 of the Gospel according to St. Luke.


## Chapter V

1 Jacques Ellul, *The Meaning of the City* (Grand Rapids: Eerdmans Publishing Co., 1970), pp. 149, 154.

2 *Ibid.*

3 Mumford makes a very strong case for this in *The Pentagon of Power,* Chapter 2, "Return of the Sun God."

4 Jacques Ellul, *The Meaning of the City.*

5 Peter De Vries, *Mrs. Wallop* (Boston: Little, Brown, 1970).

6 I am indebted to Jacques Ellul for his stimulating insights into the meaning of the story, *The Meaning of the City,* pp. 15-20.

7 See esp. Chapter XI in *The Greening of America.*

8 *The Pentagon of Power,* p. 433.


## Chapter VI

1 *The Children of Light and the Children of Darkness,* p. xi.

2 *The Greening of America,* pp. 88, 90. See Chapter V throughout.

3 Herbert Marcuse, *One Dimensional Man* (Boston: Beacon Press, 1966; Paperback Ed.), p. 1.

4 *Ibid.,* p. 3.

5 Reinhold Niebuhr, *The Irony of American History* (New York: Charles Scribner's Sons, 1952), p. 93.

6 *The Pentagon of Power,* pp. 15-16.

7 *Raintree County* (Boston: Houghton Mifflin, 1958).

8 T. S. Eliot, Choruses from *The Rock, VI* in *Collected Poems 1909-1962* (New York: Harcourt, Brace & World, 1963), p. 160.

9 Daniel Moynihan, to a graduating class at Notre Dame, quoted in *The Wall Street Journal,* June 20, 1969, p. 14.

10 *The Coming World Civilization,* p. 6.

## Chapter VII

1 Erik Erikson, *Young Man Luther* (New York: W. W. Norton & Co., 1958), p. 220.

2 Henry David Thoreau, in *Walden* (New York: The New American Library of World Literature, 1962), Part I, Economy.

3 *Eros and Civilisation,* p. 13.

4 *Ibid.,* p. 58, n. 45; p. 78.

5 Peter Drucker, *The Age of Discontinuity* (New York: Harper & Row, 1968), p. 289.

6 *The Pentagon of Power,* p. 406.

7 Paul Goodman, *Growing up Absurd* (Vintage Books; New York: Random House, 1956), p. 41.

8 William A. Williams, *The Great Evasion* (Chicago: Quadrangle Books, 1968; Paperback Ed.), p. 171.

9 *Growing up Absurd,* p. 17.

10 *Ibid.,* pp. 28-29.

11 *The Greening of America,* p. 189.

12 *Ibid.,* p. 195.

13 Erik Erikson, *Identity: Youth and Crisis,* p. 127.

14 Michael Harrington, in *The Accidental Century* (New York: The Macmillan Co., 1965), pp. 254-59, traces this development, without being quite so specific as I think we must be.

15 *Young Man Luther,* p. 220.

16 *Ibid.*

**Chapter VIII**

1 *The Meaning of the City,* pp. 163, 171.
2 *Insight and Responsibility,* p. 115.
3 *Ibid.,* p. 140. See the entire essay "Human Strength and the Cycle of Generations," *ibid.,* pp. 109-57.
4 Oscar Cullmann has made a brief and rather representative study of this question in *Immortality of the Soul or Resurrection of the Dead?* (London: Epworth Press, 1956).
5 Northrop Frye, *The Stubborn Structure* (Ithaca, N.Y.: Cornell University Press, 1970), p. 120.
6 *The Children of Light and the Children of Darkness,* pp. 118, 145.
7 See the quotation at the beginning of this chapter.